Michael Hayk [illegible] arefully researched and [illegible] knowl-edges that faith [illegible] ice and passionately asse[illegible] the urgent need for recovering this among evangelical pastors—and, I would quickly add, professors as well. This volume seeks to rekindle the love for one another grounded in Christ, with Christ, and for Christ for advancing God's kingdom. I strongly commend its value and trust all those who read it will intentionally apply these words to their own lives!

Tom Schwanda is associate professor emeritus of Christian Formation and Ministry, Wheaton College, Wheaton, IL

This informative book on friendship is a refreshing corrective to the increasing individualism among many today, including Christians. This volume raises the bar on our understanding of Christian friendship. As stated, true friendship is a means of grace for our mutual benefit. The author is a skilled historian who effectively illustrates his important thesis by drawing mostly from letters between eighteenth-century British pastors. Further, Michael Haykin is well suited to write about the value and necessity of Christian friendship, for his life exemplifies it.

Grant Gordon is the editor of *Wise Counsel: John Newton's Letters to John Ryland Jr.* and author of *A Great Blessing to Me: John Newton Encounters George Whitefield*

Haykin ably extracts the vital theme of friendship from his deep acquaintance with eighteenth-century Particular Baptists, and Christian history more generally. His investigation is contextually grounded, elucidated by many historical anecdotes and enveloped in the warmth of biblical spirituality. Thus, *Iron Sharpens Iron* is a practical and academically rich historical inquiry into an often underappreciated area (i.e., friendship) and a contemporary challenge to the individualism and isolationism of modern evangelicalism. Truly, friendship is not only a means of grace; as Haykin argues, it is a gift of grace.

Christopher W. Crocker is the pastor of Markdale Baptist Church, ON, and adjunct professor of church history at Toronto Baptist Seminary, Toronto, ON

This is a wonderful book on spiritual friendship. It speaks to an age which, as Michael Haykin says, is more interested in getting and possessing than sacrificing and giving. Ironically, we end up greatly impoverished as a result. Professor Haykin draws on the riches of the past to challenge and inspire us, giving us models to draw from as we build and nurture healthy, godly friendships today. I know this is a subject close to the author's heart, and I cannot think of anyone better qualified to write this book. *Iron Sharpens Iron* could change not only your life but also the lives of those around you.

Peter J. Morden is the senior pastor of Cornerstone Baptist Church, Leeds, and Distinguished Visiting Scholar, Spurgeon's College, London, England

Our culture's obsessions have driven much that is beautiful from the world. For example, radical individualism and the hyper-sexualization of human relations have deprived us of the ability to nurture deep friendships. C. S. Lewis said that in practical terms, friendship, like philosophy and art, has no "survival value." However, he went on to say that "it is one of those things which give value to survival." Michael Haykin's book *Iron Sharpens Iron* provides a welcome remedy to the contemporary de-valuing of friendship. Haykin draws on the profound history of Christian spirituality and roots the subject in biblical truth. This book will bless you and encourage you to catch up with an old friend.

Samuel E. Masters is the rector of Seminario Biblico William Carey, Córdoba, Argentina

Union

Michael A.G. Haykin

IRON SHARPENS IRON

Friendship and the grace of God

Iron Sharpens Iron: Friendship and the Grace of God

www.UnionPublishing.org
Bridgend, United Kingdom

Cover and book design by Rubner Durais

ISBN 978-1-9168995-1-3 (paperback)
ISBN 978-1-9168995-3-7(eBook)

"True friendship is the noblest earthly gift
Which heaven on man bestows ...
Not mines afford a gem of equal worth."

— Anne Steele,
from *Poems on Subjects Chiefly Devotional* (1780)

To five dear Canadian friends
who have made the subject-matter of this book
a precious reality in my life:

Dave Barker
Ian Clary
Heinz Dschankilic
Tyler Flatt
Kirk Wellum

CONTENTS

Introduction 13

1 Friendship in the West: From Antiquity to the Age of Reason 21

2 Who Were Andrew Fuller and John Ryland? 41

3 To "take sweet counsel together": The Friendship of John Newton and John Ryland 59

4 "We must … be together as much as possible": The Friendship of Andrew Fuller and Thomas Steevens 77

Excursus: A "once intimate friend": How the friendship of Edward Sharman and Andrew Fuller ended 107

5 "A fountain of sweets": The Friendship of Andrew Fuller and John Ryland & Robert Hall's Mini-discourse on Friendship 111

Appendix: Lemuel Covell and His Letter on Christian Friendship (1801) 131

For Further Reading 139

Acknowledgements 143

INTRODUCTION

On Wednesday, October 23, 1782, John Collett Ryland (1723–1792) sat down in either his home in Northampton or his church, College Lane Baptist Church, to finish the preface to a new work he had written on the deity of Christ. The preface not only described what Ryland had sought to achieve in this book, but also mentioned plans that Ryland had for a further volume on the Holy Spirit. A pressing reason in Ryland's mind for the latter was his observation that "in the present age, there is a peculiar and dreadful enmity to the divinity, personality, and work of the Holy Spirit."[1]

Ryland did not spell out what he meant by this remark, and it remains a somewhat cryptic observation. Was he talking mainly about the eighteenth-century rise of rationalism in the form of Deism and Socinianism, that is, Unitarianism?

1 John [Collett] Ryland, *Contemplations on the Divinity of Christ, Evinced from His Names Jehovah, God, and Sovereign Lord; His Attributes and Actions, the Beauties of Creation, Providence, and Redemption; and the Acts of Worship Paid to Him in Scripture* (Northampton: Thomas Dicey and Co., 1783), 3:ix.

Or did he have in view primarily the scorn of the ruling classes and intellectual elite of Georgian England for the evangelical awakenings as forms of "enthusiasm," that is, fanaticism?

Whatever Ryland meant exactly by this statement, it bears witness to a profound conviction that he and his fellow Baptists had with regard to the Holy Spirit: they were adamant that keeping in step with the Spirit was *the* vital matter when it came to the nourishment of the soul of the believer or the inner life of a congregation. As John Sutcliff (1752–1814) of Olney, Buckinghamshire—a close friend of Ryland's son, John Ryland, Jr. (1753–1825)—observed:

> The outpouring of the divine Spirit ... is the grand promise of the New Testament ... His influences are the soul, the great animating soul of all religion. These withheld, divine ordinances are empty cisterns, and spiritual graces are withering flowers. These suspended, the greatest human abilities labour in vain, and the noblest efforts fail of success.[2]

Yet, these Baptists were also certain that to seek the Spirit's strength apart from various means through which the Spirit was known to work was both unbiblical and foolish. Among these spiritual disciplines or means of grace, which included ones that Christians today would likely enumerate such as prayer and preaching, was friendship. As another of the younger Ryland's friends, Robert Hall, Jr. (1764–1831), put it:

---

2 John Sutcliff, *Jealousy for the Lord of Hosts, Illustrated* (London: W. Button, 1791), 12.

> Next to the immediate guidance of God by his Spirit, the counsel and encouragement of virtuous and enlightened friends afford the most powerful aid, in the encounter of temptation and in the career of duty. ... [Friendship] is ... a reserve of strength, ready to be called into action when most needed; a fountain of sweets, to which we may continually repair, whose waters are inexhaustible.[3]

How vastly different is this perspective on friendship from that of both Western culture and Western Christianity. Modern culture in the West is not one that provides great encouragement for the nurture and development of deep, long-lasting, satisfying friendships. Such friendships take time and sacrifice, and the West in the early twenty-first century is a busy, busy world that, generally speaking, is far more interested in getting and possessing than sacrificing and giving.[4] Moreover, during the course of the twentieth century, popular Western culture "developed an obsession with individual selfhood and sexual desire that marginalized friendship."[5]

What is especially disturbing about this fact is that Western Anglophone Christianity is far too often little

---

3 Robert Hall, Jr., *A Sermon Occasioned by the Death of the Rev. John Ryland, D.D., Preached at the Baptist Meeting, Broadmead, Bristol, June 5, 1825*, in *The Works of the Rev. Robert Hall, A.M.*, ed. Olinthus Gregory, 2nd ed. (London: Holdsworth and Ball, 1832), 1:378, 380.

4 Diogenes Allen, *Love: Christian Romance, Marriage, Friendship* (Cambridge, MA: Cowley Publications, 1987), 45–46.

5 Ivy Schweitzer, *Perfecting Friendship: Politics and Affiliation in Early American Literature* (Chapel Hill, NC: University of North Carolina Press, 2006), 10. Alan Jacobs believes that the emergence of the modern perspective on friendship began during the transition from the Enlightenment to Romanticism. See his "Friendship and Its Discontents," *First Things* 28 (December 1992): 43.

different from its cultural setting. The English Anglican writer C. S. Lewis (1898–1963) wrote an ingenious little book entitled *The Screwtape Letters,* a remarkable commentary on spiritual warfare from the point of view of our enemy. In it, there is one letter from the senior devil, Screwtape, to his nephew, Wormwood, in which Screwtape rejoices over the fact that "in modern Christian writings" there is to be found "few of the old warnings about Worldly Vanities, the Choice of Friends, and the Value of Time."[6]

Now, whether or not Lewis is right with regard to a scarcity of modern Christian literature about "Worldly Vanities" and "the Value of Time," he is undoubtedly correct when it comes to the topic of friendship. Indeed, until fairly recently, it was difficult to find contemporary evangelical works on this vital topic.[7] Jaroslav Pelikan has rightly observed in this regard that modern works of Christian theology have not found "an appropriate category for the meaning of friendship." As he went on to note: "It would seem safe to say, even without the empirical evidence of a word count, that in manuals of theology and canon law references to disciples past and present as 'servants' outnumber references to them as 'friends' by a factor of fifty or a hundred."[8] In a book review, Alan Jacobs makes a similar observation and pointedly asks, "Why are there so few attempts, by Christians anyway ... to formulate a theology of friendship?"[9]

---

6 C. S. Lewis, *The Screwtape Letters,* Letter 10 in *The Best of C. S. Lewis* (Washington, DC: Canon Press, 1969), 43.

7 See "For Further Reading" below.

8 Jaroslav Pelikan, "Friendship" in his *Melody of Theology: A Philosophical Dictionary* (Cambridge, MA; London: Harvard University Press, 1988), 93.

9 Jacobs, "Friendship and Its Discontents," 46.

A personal anecdote is germane here. About twenty-five years ago, when I was teaching full-time at Heritage Seminary in Cambridge, Ontario, I told a fellow faculty member of a piece of advice that W. Gordon Brown (1904–1979), the founding Dean of Central Baptist Seminary in Toronto, used to give to prospective pastors. I never met Dean Brown, who died a few years before I began teaching. But I had heard that he used to advise students who were hoping to become pastors to avoid developing close friendships with any of their parishioners in the churches that they pastored. I vividly recall relating this in the mid-1990s to a fellow faculty member at Heritage, who, to my shock and horror, told me that he advised students to not even form friendships with fellow pastors, for, this individual told me, they would use whatever confidences you shared with them against you. Maybe he had had a bad experience in this regard. Be this as it may, I have long considered this as illustrative of the low esteem in which friendship is held among certain evangelicals.

This book makes a case for seeing friendship as Baptists and others in the eighteenth century saw it: as a vital means of grace in the Christian life. The first chapter looks at some highlights in the history of friendship, spanning the ancient world to the eighteenth-century Age of Reason, and, as such, lays out its importance for previous generations. Chapters 3–5 examine three friendships that revolve around two eighteenth-century men, the Baptist pastor-theologians Andrew Fuller (1754–1815) and John Ryland, Jr., whose lives are summarized in Chapter 2.

In particular, Chapter 3 considers the intergenerational friendship between John Ryland and John Newton

(1725–1807), who, in many ways, was both a father figure and sage friend to Ryland. Then, in Chapter 4, we look at eight letters from Andrew Fuller to his fellow Baptist pastor Thomas Steevens (1745–1802) to see how a central medium of the eighteenth century, the letter, served as the glue of a friendship that Fuller clearly regarded as an intimate one. But not all friendships flourish, as I detail in an excursus on the collapse of the friendship of Andrew Fuller and Edward Sharman (fl. 1770–1800). Finally, in Chapter 5, we turn to the friendship of Fuller and Ryland, which stretched over thirty-nine years and only ended in this world with the death of Fuller. This chapter also includes a discussion of an extended discourse on friendship in this Baptist community—namely, a portion of the funeral sermon for Ryland that was preached by Robert Hall, Jr. (1764–1831).[10]

Throughout this volume, I have purposely not argued my case for the vital necessity of friendship in the Christian life by means of philosophical or theological reflection. I have focused instead on the historical evidence and fruit of tangible interactions between actual friends. Though I have concentrated on only three friendships, a number of others from this era and denominational context could well have been examined.[11] It is on the grounds of these men's experience of

10 For a broader use of the term "friendship" by an eighteenth-century Baptist author, see the Appendix.

11 These include the friendships of John Beddome and Bernard Foskett, Benjamin Francis and Joshua Thomas, Caleb Evans and John Ash, and David and Joseph Kinghorn. See also Jacob P. Salley, "'I loved him as a most affectionate brother': Friendship in the Life and Thought of Caleb Evans (1737–1791)" (Advanced M.Div. thesis, The Southern Baptist Theological Seminary, 2018). On recovering a Baptist theology of friendship, see Thomas R. McKibbens, "Ministry as Friendship; or, How South Carolina Created a New Model," *Journal of the South Carolina Baptist Historical Society* 25 (November 1999): 2–9.

the joys and challenges of Christian friendship that I seek to make my case.

A final note concerns the term "means of grace." Baptists in the eighteenth century recognized various ways in which God the Holy Spirit worked in human lives: through the Word that he had inspired the prophets and the apostles to write; through the ordinances of baptism and the Lord's Supper; through prayer. And he also worked, in their minds, through the bonds of Christian friendship. Of course, the latter did not automatically bestow grace, but they were viewed as one way or means by which the Holy Spirit's gracious presence sanctified believers and enabled them to persevere in Christ. *Iron Sharpens Iron* is about the specific way that friendship functioned as a means of grace for two eighteenth-century men, Andrew Fuller and John Ryland.[12]

12 Alan Jacobs curiously states that "when one tries to think of great Christian friendships, few come to mind." And among the few that he lists is the friendship of John Newton and William Cowper ("Friendship and Its Discontents," 45–46). I suspect that Jacobs is using the word "great" here as a synonym for "famous." As I hope to demonstrate in these pages, some of the eighteenth-century friendships that I discuss are indeed "great Christian friendships" and should be much better known.

Chapter 1

FRIENDSHIP IN THE WEST: FROM ANTIQUITY TO THE AGE OF REASON

> "Friendship affords the highest and most sweet enjoyment that is to be had in this life, or that rational creatures are capable of."
>
> Samuel Hopkins,
> *A Discourse on Christian Friendship* (1767)

In a masterful study of the various ways in which English society between the time of the Reformation in the sixteenth century and the Enlightenment in the eighteenth century sought to find fulfillment and so define human flourishing, historian Keith Thomas devotes an entire chapter to those close personal relationships that fall under the rubric of "friendship."[1] As Thomas traces the history of friendship in

1 Keith Thomas, *The Ends of Life: Roads to Fulfilment in Early Modern England* (Oxford: Oxford University Press, 2009), 187–225.

this period of English history, he notes that it came to be based "wholly on mutual sympathy, and cherished for its own sake rather than for its practical advantages." Friends were understood to be "intimate companions, freely chosen, without regard to an ulterior end,"[2] which Keith sees as a significant development in the history of friendship.

John Flaxman (1755–1826), "Achilles and Patroclus"
(Art Institute of Chicago, public domain, PICRYL)

FRIENDSHIP IN ANTIQUITY

Yet, reflections on friendship as far back as the Greco-Roman era, for example, recognized the importance of such affection as foundational to being human rather than as merely a means to another end such as subsistence, security, or social advancement. At the fountainhead of Western literature are the Bible and the Greek masterpieces by Homer, *The Iliad* and *The Odyssey*.

2 Thomas, *The Ends of Life*, 187–225, *passim*.

One of the major themes of *The Iliad* is friendship. For example, when Patroclus, the closest friend of the warrior Achilles, has been slain, Achilles exclaimed that Patroclus was the man "whom I revered beyond all my companions, as equal to my own life."[3] It was Achilles' undying love for his friend that fueled his anger and desire to revenge Patroclus' death by slaying his killer, Hector.

Indeed, friendship was deemed to be of such vital importance among the Greeks that the Athenian philosopher Plato (*c.* 420s–348/347 BC) devoted an entire book, the *Lysis*, as well as substantial portions of two other books, the *Phaedrus* and the *Symposium*, to a treatment of its nature. Aristotle (384–322 BC), the other leading thinker of the classical Greek period, also considered the topic of friendship significant enough to have a discussion of it occupy two of the ten books of the *Nicomachean Ethics*, his major work on ethical issues. For the ancient Greeks—and this is true also of the Romans—friendship formed one of the highest ideals of human life.[4]

FRIENDSHIP IN THE BIBLE

While the Bible does not contain an extended discussion of the concept of friendship as we find in the writings of Plato or Aristotle, there are important reflections on friendship

3 Homer, *Iliad* 18.81–82, trans. Caroline Alexander, *The Iliad* (New York, NY: CCCO, 2015), 393.

4 See the discussions of E. D. H. (Liz) Carmichael, *Friendship: Interpreting Christian Love* (London; New York: T&T Clark International, 2004), 7–22; Douglas A. Hume, *The Early Christian Community: A Narrative Analysis of Acts 2:41–47 and 4:32–35* (Tübingen: Mohr Siebeck, 2011), 44–77. On Aristotle's view of friendship, see especially Kevin Vost, *The Four Friendships: From Aristotle to Aquinas* (Brooklyn, NY: Angelico Press, 2018), 13–59.

(see Eccl. 4:9–12) as well as marvelous illustrations of good friendship—for instance, those of Ruth and Naomi or David and Jonathan. The Old Testament compendium of wisdom, Proverbs, includes occasional nuggets of advice about having and keeping friends. In Proverbs 17:17, for example, we are told that a true "friend loves at all times," while in Proverbs 18:24 we are reminded that "there is a friend who sticks closer than a brother."[5] Such texts as these leave the reader with the distinct impression that the world of the Bible regards friendship as a very important part of life.[6]

The Bible uses two significant images in its representation of friendship.[7] The first is the knitting together of souls. Deuteronomy provides the earliest use of this image, where a friend is described as one who is "as your own soul" (Deut. 13:6), that is, a companion of one's innermost thoughts and feelings. The same idea recurs in 1 Samuel 18:1, where we read that "the soul of Jonathan was knit to the soul of David, and Jonathan loved him as his own soul." The privileges and responsibilities of a biblical friend involve intimacy, loyalty, and a strong emotional attachment.[8]

---

5 For a helpful study of friendship in Proverbs, see Bruce Waltke, "Friends and Friendship in the Book of Proverbs: An Exposition of Proverbs 27:1–22," *Crux* 38, no. 3 (September 2002): 27–42.

6 *Pace* Gary McGonagill, "'Becoming Aware of Himself, He Sought a Friend': Friendship, Grief, and Wisdom in *The Epic of Gilgamesh* and *The Iliad*" in Susan Harris, ed., *Christian Friendship: Papers Delivered at the Twenty-Fifth Annual Atlantic Theological Conference, June 26th to 29th, 2005, Anglican Diocesan Centre, Halifax, Nova Scotia* (Charlottetown, PE: St. Peter Publications, 2005), 82: "Human friendship in the story of David and Jonathan is not ... of itself a proper object of narrative attention [in the Bible], as it was felt to be by both the Greeks and Mesopotamians."

7 "Friendship," *Dictionary of Biblical Imagery*, ed. Leland Ryken et al. (Downers Grove, IL; Leicester: InterVarsity Press, 1998), 308–309.

8 R. Paul Stevens, "Friendship" in Robert Banks and R. Paul Stevens, eds., *The*

The second image that the Bible uses to represent friendship is the face-to-face encounter. This is the image used for Moses' relationship to God. We are told that in the tabernacle, God spoke to Moses "face to face, as a man speaks to his friend" (Exod. 33:11).[9] This depiction of friendship as a face-to-face encounter implies conversation, a sharing of confidences, and consequently, a meeting of minds, goals, and direction. One of the benefits of face-to-face encounters between friends is the heightened insight that such encounters produce. A proverb that highlights this idea is the famous one from Proverbs 27:17, "Iron sharpens iron, and one man sharpens another."[10]

THE FRIENDSHIP OF PAUL AND TIMOTHY

Another of the great friendships of the Bible is that of Paul and Timothy. A close reading of the Pauline corpus reveals that Paul is a man rarely found without companions. Samuel Johnson (1709–1784), the eighteenth-century author and lexicographer, once said about his friend Sir John Hawkins that he was "a most unclubbable man." Such a remark could not be said of Paul. He was very "clubbable," a gregarious man, who "delighted in the company of his fellows."[11] And of his companions, the dearest would have to have been Timothy. Though he was probably twenty or so years Paul's junior, Timothy became the

---

Complete Book of Everyday Christianity (Downers Grove, IL: InterVarsity Press, 1997), 439. For an example of this kind of friendship in the New Testament, see John 11:11, 35–36.

9 See also Numbers 12:8.

10 For Andrew Fuller's use of this proverb to describe himself, see below.

11 F. F. Bruce, *Paul: Apostle of the Heart Set Free* (Grand Rapids, MI: Eerdmans, 1977), 457.

apostle's closest friend. In the words of F. F. Bruce, Timothy "readily surrendered whatever personal ambitions he might have cherished in order to play the part of a son to Paul and help him in his missionary activity, showing a selfless concern for others that matched the apostle's own eagerness to spend and be spent for them."[12]

Timothy had joined the Pauline circle in what is termed Paul's second missionary journey, that is, around 48 or 49.[13] Over the next number of years, Timothy's soul began to mirror that of Paul, and his mind became increasingly attuned to the wavelengths of the apostle's thinking. Thus, Timothy's friendship with Paul would have been a means by which God sanctified the younger man, giving him an ever-increasing richness of thought about God and the gospel and an ever-growing desire for holiness and conformity to Christ.

In 1 Corinthians 15:33, Paul urged the Corinthians to recognize that "bad company corrupts good morals" (CSB). Intimate friendships with evil characters will invariably have a negative effect on our lives. Likewise, one can say that "good company promotes good habits." This was the effect that Paul would undoubtedly have had on Timothy. As Maurice Roberts has put it: "Our best friends are those whose company most makes us afraid to sin."[14]

---

12 Bruce, *Paul*, 457.

13 Acts 16:1–3. As he traveled with Paul, Timothy had firsthand experience of Paul's "teaching, conduct, purpose [in life], faith, patience, love, and endurance, along with ... persecutions and sufferings" (2 Tim. 3:10–11 CSB).

14 Maurice Roberts, *The Thought of God* (Edinburgh: The Banner of Truth Trust, 1993), 176.

Probably the clearest text in which the dearness of Paul's friendship with Timothy comes out is Philippians 2:19–22. Evidently, the Philippian church had been experiencing some measure of disunity. Paul mentioned it explicitly in chapter 4 when he urges Euodia and Syntyche "to be like-minded in the Lord" (v. 2, my translation). In chapter 2, Paul devoted a lengthy section of this letter to resolving this problem. He began by urging the Philippians to be "likeminded"—the same phrase that Paul employed in Philippians 4:2—"having the same love, being of one accord, of one mind," looking out for not only their own interests but also those of others (Phil. 2:2, 4 KJV).

To illustrate this admonition and drive it home, Paul encouraged the Philippians to meditate on the example of Christ, whose mind and heart were focused not on his own personal interests but on those of fallen humanity. So taken up was Christ with the lot of sinners that though he was fully God, he "made himself of no reputation" (Phil. 2:7 KJV). He became incarnate, and, willingly and humbly, he took upon himself the burden of human sin; he was "obedient to the point of death, even the death of the cross" (v. 8 ESV).

After he had outlined the work and motivation of Christ, the apostle Paul did not leave this theme of thinking of others' best interests. In Philippians 2:19–22, he gave a second example of being like-minded and having the interests of others at heart. This time, he turned to his friend Timothy:

> I trust in the Lord Jesus to send Timothy to you shortly, that I also may be encouraged when I know your state. For I have no one like-minded, who will sincerely care for your state. For all seek their own, not the things which are of Christ Jesus. But you know his proven character, that as a son with his father he served with me in the gospel. (NKJV)

From the words and phrases that Paul used here, it is clear that he was recommending Timothy as an example of Christlikeness. Unlike others that Paul knew, Timothy sincerely cared for the state of the Philippians. He was genuinely concerned about the needs of other believers and was not solely seeking to promote his own interests. In other words, he displayed the mind of Christ. Paul could thus describe him in verse 20 as "like-minded": because of his desire to be like Christ, Timothy was one who fully shared Paul's heart and mind. As such, he was a completely trustworthy companion and friend of Paul.[15]

Due to their age difference, Paul naturally spoke of Timothy as his "son," as he went on to say that Timothy had proven his worth during his ministry with Paul "as a son with his father." But he quickly added that Timothy had not been *his* servant; instead, he had been serving the gospel. Paul was always very careful to avoid giving the impression that he was lord and master over the faith of others. Timothy did not serve him, but together as equals before God they served the Lord of the gospel, Christ. In this text from Philippians, we see

15 Panayotis Christou, "ΙΣΟΨΥΧΟΣ, Phil. 2:20," *The Journal of Biblical Literature* 70 (1951): 293–296.

clearly the way that Paul prized his friendship with Timothy and the way that it was based on a harmony of heart and mind. Without such harmony, there can be no intimate friendship.

Jean Bondol (fl. 1368–1381), "Paul sending a letter to Timothy" (National Library of the Netherlands, public domain, PICRYL)

The final record of this friendship is found in 2 Timothy. This letter was written weeks, perhaps a few months, before Paul's death by a Roman executioner. As he wrote, Paul was in a cell in an obscure prison in Rome, while Timothy was in Ephesus, on the coast of what is today modern Turkey. Paul opened the letter by describing Timothy as a "beloved son" (2 Tim. 1:2 KJV) whom he regularly remembered in prayer and whom he eagerly desired to see. As he thought of Timothy, he especially recalled the last time that the two were together, when Timothy broke down and wept (vv. 2–4). This occasion may well have been when Paul was arrested.

After encouraging Timothy to hold fast to the gospel, to pursue godliness, and to fulfill his ministry in 2 Timothy 1–3, Paul told his friend of his impending death. He faced this prospect with confidence, aware that he was saved and in a right relationship with "the righteous judge" (2 Tim. 4:6–8).

But so strong was his friendship with Timothy that Paul had no sooner mentioned his imminent death than he urged Timothy to "make every effort to come to me soon" (2 Tim. 4:9 CSB). In fact, as Paul drew the letter to a close, he again urged his friend: "Make every effort to come before winter" (2 Tim. 4:21 CSB). During the winter months from November to March, it was dangerous to sail the Mediterranean, and much of the shipping in that region halted. Aware of this and conscious that his death was close, Paul was here urging Timothy to sail from Ephesus for Rome before the winter months. If Timothy failed to leave before the shipping lanes closed, then he would have to travel overland to Rome, which would take considerably longer, and he would arrive in Rome after Paul's death. So precious is this friendship to Paul that he wished to see his dear friend one last time before his eyes closed in death.

Did Timothy go to Rome? Well, there is an intriguing verse in the final chapter of Hebrews, in which the unknown author of that letter stated, "Be aware that our brother Timothy has been released" (Heb. 13:23 CSB). It would seem that at this point in time, Timothy has been in prison and has just been released. Did this imprisonment result from Timothy's going to Rome to see his dear friend one final time in this world? If so, it is an imprisonment that Timothy suffered for the sake of friendship.

CHRISTIAN FRIENDSHIPS

It is instructive to observe that the spread of the church throughout the Roman Empire in the centuries immediately after the death of Paul did not negate the rich appreciation of friendship that is evident in the Bible. Despite the Christian emphasis on showing love to *all* men and women—family, friends, acquaintances, even enemies—friendship continued to be highly valued. In fact, the emphasis placed on the unity in Christ of all Christians encouraged a high degree of spiritual intimacy that resembled, and even surpassed, the intimacy considered by Greco-Roman paganism to be essential to the experience of genuine friendship.[16]

The Cappadocian theologian Gregory of Nazianzus (*c.* 329–389), for example, wrote of his friendship with his fellow Cappadocian Basil of Caesarea (*c.* 330–379) during their time together as students in Athens in the 350s:

> In studies, in lodgings, in discussions I had him as companion. ... We had all things in common, ... But above all it was God, of course, and a mutual desire for higher things, that drew us to each other. As a result we reached such a pitch of confidence that we revealed the depths of our hearts, becoming ever more united in our yearning.[17]

---

16 Carolinne White, *Christian Friendship in the Fourth Century* (Cambridge: Cambridge University Press, 1992), 57.

17 Gregory of Nazianzus, *On His Life*, trans. Denise Molaise Meehan, *Saint Gregory of Nazianzus: Three Poems*, The Fathers of the Church, vol. 75 (Washington, DC: The Catholic University of America Press, 1987), 83–84.

Given this estimation of friendship, it is no surprise that Gregory also stated: "If anyone were to ask me, 'What is the best thing in life?' I would answer, 'Friends.'"[18]

Alan Jacobs has observed that there is "no greater and more moving passage about friendship" than that of Augustine's (354–430) description in book 4 of his *Confessions*.[19] It is Augustine's account of the death of an extremely close friend whom he had known since childhood. This was a relationship, Augustine noted, that was "sweeter to me than all the joys of life."[20] But, as Augustine had come to realize by the time that he wrote the *Confessions* at the close of the fourth century, "No friends are true friends unless you, my God, bind them fast to one another through that love which is sown in our hearts by the Holy Spirit, who is given to us."[21] Thus Augustine was led to compose this blessing: "Blessed are those who love you, O God, and love their friends in you…"[22]

In the Middle Ages, Aelred of Rievaulx (1110–1167), an English Cistercian monk, penned a classic on this subject, *Spiritual Friendship*. For Aelred, who in this regard is clearly

18 As quoted in White, *Christian Friendship in the Fourth Century*, 70.

19 Alan Jacobs, "Friendship and Its Discontents," *First Things* 28 (December 1992): 42.

20 Augustine, *Confessions* 4.4, trans. R. S. Pine-Coffin, *Confessions* (London: Penguin Books, 1961), 75. For the entirety of this mini-reflection on friendship, see *Confessions* 4.4–9. See also Augustine, *Letter 258*.

For secondary studies, see especially Donald V. Burt, *Friendship and Society: An Introduction to Augustine's Practical Philosophy* (Grand Rapids, MI; Cambridge: Eerdmans, 1999) and Coleman Michael Ford, "'A Bond Between Souls': Understanding Spiritual Friendship in Augustine of Hippo with Special Reference to his Letters" (Ph.D. thesis, The Southern Baptist Theological Seminary, 2019). I am also indebted to Profs. Coleman Ford and Ian Clary for this note and discussion of Augustine's view of friendship.

21 Augustine, *Confessions* 4.4, trans. Pine-Coffin, *Confessions*, 75, altered. Augustine is clearly alluding to Romans 5:5, one of his favorite Pauline texts.

22 Augustine, *Confessions* 4.9, trans. Pine-Coffin, *Confessions*, 79.

indebted to Augustine, genuine friendship must "begin in Christ, continue in Christ, and be perfected in Christ." Such spiritual friendship is to be highly prized: "In human affairs nothing more sacred is striven for, nothing more useful is sought after, nothing more difficult is discovered, nothing more sweet experienced, and nothing more profitably possessed [than friendship]. For friendship bears fruit in this life and in the next."[23]

At the beginning of the modern era, John Calvin (1509–1564), who has an undeserved reputation of being harsh and unloving, also had a rich appreciation of friendship. The French Reformed historian Richard Stauffer reckoned that there were few men at the time of the Reformation "who developed as many friendships" as Calvin.[24] Two of his closest friends were his fellow Reformers Guillaume Farel (1489–1565) and Pierre Viret (1511–1571). Calvin celebrated his friendship with these two men in his preface to his *Commentary on Titus*, where he stated:

> I do not believe that there have ever been such friends who have lived together in such a deep friendship in their everyday style of life in this world as we have in our ministry. I have served here in the office of pastor with you two. There was never any appearance of envy; it seems to me

23 Aelred of Rievaulx, *Spiritual Friendship* 1.9; 2.9, trans. Mary Eugenia Laker (Kalamazoo, MI: Cistercian Publications, 1977), 53, 71. On Aelred's view of friendship, see especially Brian Patrick McGuire, *Friendship & Community: The Monastic Experience 350–1250*, Cistercian Studies Series, no. 95 (Kalamazoo, MI: Cistercian Publications, 1988), 296–338; Carmichael, *Friendship*, 70–100; and Vost, *Four Friendships*, 97–138.

24 Richard Stauffer, *The Humanness of John Calvin*, trans. George H. Shriver (Nashville, TN: Abingdon Press, 1971), 47.

> that you two and I were as one person. ... And we have shown through visible witness and good authority before men that we have among us no other understanding or friendship than that which has been dedicated to the name of Christ, has been to the present time of profit to his church, and has no other purpose but that all may be one in him with us.[25]

This brotherly friendship is best expressed in the correspondence of these three men, from which we have 163 extant letters from Calvin to Farel, 137 from Farel to Calvin, 204 letters from Calvin to Viret, and 185 from Viret to Calvin.

To note but one example that illustrates the truth of Proverbs 27:17, cited earlier ("Iron sharpens iron, and one man sharpens another"), on January 27, 1552, Calvin wrote to Farel and chided him for reports that he had heard—true reports, apparently—about the undue length of Farel's sermons. "You have frequently confessed," Calvin reminded his friend, "that you were aware of this defect, and that you were endeavouring to correct it." Calvin went on to encourage Farel to shorten his sermons lest Satan use Farel's failing in this regard to destroy the many good things being produced by his ministry.[26]

25 As quoted in Stauffer, *Humanness of Calvin*, 57.

26 John Calvin, Letter to Guillaume Farel, January 27, 1552, in his *Tracts and Letters*, ed. Jules Bonnet and trans. David Constable (1858, Edinburgh; Carlisle, PA: The Banner of Truth Trust, 2009), 5:337. For a study of Calvin's friendships, see especially Machiel A. van den Berg, *Friends of Calvin*, trans. Reinder Bruinsma (Grand Rapids, MI: Eerdmans, 2009).

Guillaume Farel and John Calvin, The Reformation Wall, Geneva (Photograph, Michael A.G. Haykin)

TWO EIGHTEENTH-CENTURY FRIENDS

When we come to the eighteenth century—the main historical context for this book—Esther Edwards Burr (1732–1758), the third daughter of the New England divine Jonathan Edwards (1703–1758), was certain that

> Nothing is more refreshing to the soul (except communication with God himself) than the company and society

> of a friend—one that has the spirit of, and relish for, true friendship—this is becoming [to] the rational soul—this is God-like.[27]

She told her closest friend, Sarah Prince (1728–1771), the daughter of Thomas Prince, pastor of Boston's Old South Church and a close friend of Esther's father:

> I should highly value (as you my dear do) such charming friends as you have about you—friends that one might unbosom their whole soul to. ... I esteem religious conversation one of the best helps to keep up religion in the soul, excepting secret devotion, I don't know but the very best—Then what a lamentable thing that 'tis so neglected by Gods [*sic*] own children.[28]

For the Christian, true friends are those with whom one can share the deepest things of one's life. They are people with whom one can be transparent and open. In Esther's words, they are people to whom one can "unbosom [one's] whole soul."

In the course of conversation about spiritual things, the believer can find strength and encouragement for living the Christian life. In referring to spiritual conversation with

---

27 Carol F. Karlsen and Laurie Crumpacker, eds., *The Journal of Esther Edwards Burr 1754–1757* (New Haven, CT; London: Yale University Press, 1984), 185. In this quote and subsequent quotes from Esther's journal, her spelling and capitalization have been modernized. For a very brief biographical sketch of Esther, see Gerald R. McDermott, "Burr, Esther Edwards" in Donald M. Lewis, *The Blackwell Dictionary of Evangelical Biography 1730–1860* (Oxford; Cambridge, MA: Blackwell, 1995), 1:175.

28 Karlsen and Crumpacker, ed., *Journal of Esther Edwards Burr*, 112.

friends as "one of the best helps to keep up religion in the soul," Esther obviously viewed it as a means of grace, one of the ways that God the Holy Spirit keeps Christians in fellowship with the Savior. As another New England Christian, Nathanael Emmons (1745–1840)—a theologian who was mentored by close followers of Jonathan Edwards—put it in one of his favorite maxims: "A man is made by his friends."[29]

Esther earnestly sought to know the presence of God in the hurly-burly of her daily life. As she did so, she came to appreciate the fact that friends are a divine gift. Writing in her diary on January 23, 1756, she was convinced:

> 'Tis ... a great mercy that we have any friends—What would this world be without 'em—A person who looks upon himself to be friendless must of all creatures be miserable in this Life—'tis the Life of Life.[30]

Esther clearly prized having Christian friends. For her, they were one of this world's greatest sources of happiness. Why did Esther put such a value upon friendship? Well, surely because she realized that Christian friends and conversation with them is vital for spiritual growth.[31]

Esther's convictions regarding friendship as a means of grace were challenged in 1756, when one of the college tutors, John Ewing (1732–1802), told her that "he did

29 As quoted in Edward A. Park, "Memoir of Nathanael Emmons; with Sketches of his Friends and Pupils" in *The Works of Nathanael Emmons, D.D.*, ed. Jacob Ide (Boston, MA: Congregational Board of Publication, 1861), 1:115.

30 Karlsen and Crumpacker, ed., *Journal of Esther Edwards Burr*, 185.

31 Nathanael Emmons similarly stated: "I value my friends amongst the richest blessings of life" (Park, "Memoir of Nathanael Emmons" in *Works of Nathanael Emmons*, ed. Ide, 1:115).

not think women knew what friendship was," since they "were hardly capable of anything so cool and rational as friendship"! Esther lost no time in rubbishing his views. As she wrote in her *Journal*: "I retorted several severe things upon him before he had time to speak again. He blushed and seemed confused ... we carried on the dispute for an hour—I talked him quite silent."[32]

Ewing probably never forgot this encounter with Edwards' formidable daughter. He is remembered today as a noted mathematician and astronomer who became the pastor of First Presbyterian Church in Philadelphia from 1759 until his death in 1802 as well as the provost of the University of Pennsylvania for the last twenty years or so of his life.[33] When he engaged with Esther Burr on the subject of friendship, though, she rightly believed that he had a poor view of women.

When Esther died in 1758, her closest friend Sarah Prince was devastated at her loss and wrote in her diary:

> My whole prospects in this world are now changed. My whole dependence for comfort in this world gone: she was dear to me as the apple of my eye—she knew and felt all my griefs. She laid out herself for my good and was ever assiduously studying it. The God of Nature had furnished her with all that I desir'd in a friend ... She was made for

32 Karlsen and Crumpacker, eds., *Journal of Esther Edwards Burr*, 257.

33 For a brief biographical sketch, see [Robert Patterson,] "Memoir," in James P. Wilson, *Selected Sermons by the Rev. John Ewing, D.D.* (Easton, PA: Thomas J. Rogers, 1812), vii–xxiv. See also the study by his great-granddaughter, Lucy E. Lee Ewing, *Dr. John Ewing and Some of His Noted Connections* (Chicago; Philadelphia; Toronto: John C. Winston Co., 1930).

> a refin'd friend. How faithful? How sincere? How open hearted? How tender how careful how disinterested—And she was mine! O the tenderness which tied our hearts! O the comfort I have enjoy'd in her for almost 7 years! O the pleasant days and nights we have spent in opening our whole souls and pouring them into each other's breasts![34]

Hopefully, Sarah found comfort in Esther's strong conviction that "true friendship is first enkindled by a spark from heaven, and heaven will never suffer it to go out, but it will burn to all eternity."[35]

CODA

Sarah Prince's words might seem excessive, but Keith Thomas notes that there is a volume of "extravagant claims for the life-enhancing value of intimate friendship" in the English-speaking world of the eighteenth century.[36] Now, Thomas' discussion of friendship does not cite any eighteenth-century Particular Baptist claims in this regard, though he could have found statements and illustrations from this community of English Dissent aplenty, especially among the circle of friends around the pastor-theologians Andrew Fuller and John Ryland, Jr., to whose lives we now turn.

34 Karlsen and Crumpacker, eds., *Journal of Esther Edwards Burr*, 307.

35 Karlsen and Crumpacker, eds., *Journal of Esther Edwards Burr*, 92.

36 Thomas, *Ends of Life*, 191–193.

Chapter 2

WHO WERE ANDREW FULLER AND JOHN RYLAND?

> "He had a heart formed for the warmest and sincerest friendship with those whose minds were congenial with his own and who were engaged in similar pursuits, and I never knew him to be weary of their company."
>
> —Ann Coles Fuller, Letter to John Ryland, Jr. (1815), speaking of her husband, Andrew Fuller

Andrew Fuller was born in February of 1754 in Wicken, a small agricultural village in the Fen country of Cambridgeshire, where his parents, Robert Fuller (1723–1781) and Philippa Gunton (1726–1816), rented a succession of dairy farms.[1] In 1761, the family moved a short distance to Soham,

1 For Fuller's life, the classic study is that of John Ryland, *The Work of Faith, the Labour of Love, and the Patience of Hope, Illustrated; in the Life and Death of the Rev. Andrew Fuller* (London: Button & Son, 1816). A second edition of this biography appeared in 1818: *The Work of Faith, the Labour of Love, and the Patience of Hope, Illustrated; in the Life and Death of the Rev. Andrew Fuller*, 2nd ed. (London: Button & Son, 1818). Citations will be taken from this second edition.

where they began to regularly attend the local Particular—that is, Calvinistic—Baptist church. The Soham church was marred by a High Calvinist mindset—what some describe today as Hyper-Calvinism—such that the preaching of the pastor, John Eve (d. 1782), never addressed the unconverted as to their spiritual estate.[2] But, by the grace of God, it was here in Soham that Fuller was genuinely born again in November 1769.

After being baptized the following spring, Fuller became a member of the church. And in 1775, at the young age of twenty-one, Fuller was called to the pastorate of this work. He stayed until 1782, when he became the pastor of the Particular Baptist congregation at Kettering, Northamptonshire, a market town in the East Midlands, where he pastored till his death in 1815. Fuller was an autodidact, but by wide admission he was also the finest theologian

---

The two best recent biographies of Fuller are those of Paul Brewster, *Andrew Fuller: Model Pastor-Theologian* (Nashville, TN: B&H Academic, 2010) and Peter J. Morden, *The Life and Thought of Andrew Fuller (1754–1815)*, Studies in Evangelical History and Thought (Milton Keynes, England: Paternoster, 2015). See also Michael A.G. Haykin, *The Armies of the Lamb: The Spirituality of Andrew Fuller*, Classics of Reformed Spirituality, vol. 3 (Dundas, ON: Joshua Press, 2001).

2 On the history of High Calvinism, see Peter Toon, *The Emergence of Hyper-Calvinism in English Nonconformity 1689–1765* (London: The Olive Tree, 1967). For the term High Calvinism rather than Hyper-Calvinism, see Geoffrey F. Nuttall, "Northamptonshire and The Modern Question: A Turning-Point in Eighteenth-Century Dissent," in his *Studies in English Dissent* (Weston Rhyn, Shropshire: Quinta Press, 2002), 207 and n.4. Fuller himself used the term "High Calvinist" in his letters to Steevens: Andrew Fuller, Letter to Thomas Steevens, June 19, 1795, in "Extracts from the Late Rev. A. Fuller's Correspondence with the Late Rev. Mr. Steevens, of Colchester," *The Baptist Magazine* 8 (1816): 495–496. For a discussion of Fuller's letters to and friendship with Steevens, see below, Chapter 4. For an excellent discussion of the different types of High Calvinism during the nineteenth century in English Baptist circles, see Kenneth A. Dix, "Varieties of High Calvinism among the Nineteenth-Century Particular Baptists," *The Baptist Quarterly* 38 (1999–2000): 56–69.

that the transatlantic Baptist community possessed in the late eighteenth and early nineteenth centuries.[3]

Andrew Fuller (Oil painting in the personal possession of Norman Hopkins, used by permission)

FULLER AS AN APOLOGIST

Fuller's time as a pastor in Soham was a decisive period for the shaping of his theological convictions. He wrestled initially with how to preach to the lost—what was then called "the Modern Question"—as he had no models from

3 The Victorian Baptist preacher C. H. Spurgeon (1834–1892), for instance, once described Fuller as the "greatest theologian" of his century (as quoted in Gilbert Laws, *Andrew Fuller: Pastor, Theologian, Ropeholder* [London: Carey Press, 1942], 127). And in the eyes of the English Baptist historian A. C. Underwood, Fuller was "the soundest and most creatively useful theologian the Particular Baptists have ever had" (*A History of the English Baptists* [London: The Baptist Union Publication Dept. (Kingsgate Press), 1947], 166).

which to learn.[4] He eventually decided to read the Gospels and the book of Acts to see how the Lord Jesus and his apostles had dealt with those who were unconverted. This not only taught him how to preach to unbelievers but also gave him a profound desire to live wholly under the authority of the infallible Scriptures. As he later said about the Bible:

> If any man venerate the authority of Scripture, he must receive it as being what it professes to be, and for all the purposes for which it professes to be written. If the Scriptures profess to be Divinely inspired, and assume to be the infallible standard of faith and practice, we must either receive them as such, or, if we would be consistent, disown the writers as imposters.[5]

It was also during this period in Soham that Fuller began a lifelong study of the works of the American theologian

---

4 For the history of the "Modern Question," see the superb overviews by Nuttall, "Northamptonshire and *The Modern Question*," 206–230 and Gerald L. Priest, "Andrew Fuller's Response to the 'Modern Question'—A Reappraisal of *The Gospel Worthy of All Acceptation*," *Detroit Baptist Seminary Journal* 6 (Fall 2001): 45–73.

5 Andrew Fuller, *The Calvinistic and Socinian Systems Examined and Compared, as to their Moral Tendency* in *The Complete Works of the Rev. Andrew Fuller*, ed. and revised Joseph Belcher (1845, Harrisonburg, VA: Sprinkle Publications, 1988), 2:196. Hereafter, this collection of Fuller's written corpus is cited simply as *Works of the Rev. Andrew Fuller*.

In the words of Jonathan Edwards Ryland, Fuller was "a man who thought for himself; who was deeply impressed with the majesty and worth of religious truth, and who when, after earnest search, he believed himself to possess it, held the conclusions he had reached with an unflinching tenacity" ("Fuller, Rev. Andrew," *The Encyclopedia Britannica*, 8th ed. [Edinburgh: Adam and Charles Black, 1856], 10:325).

Jonathan Edwards (1703–1758), whose importance in the history of Christian thought is well captured by a recent description of him as the "American Augustine."[6] Along with the Scriptures, Edwards' writings enabled Fuller to write what turned out to be the definitive answer to the Modern Question, namely, *The Gospel Worthy of All Acceptation*.[7]

This epoch-making book sought to be faithful to the central emphases of historic Calvinism while at the same time attempting to leave preachers with no alternative but to drive home to their hearers the universal obligations of repentance and faith. It was also during this period that Fuller met two men who would become lifelong friends and coworkers, John Ryland, Jr. (1753–1825), later the president of Bristol Baptist Academy, and John Sutcliff (1752–1814), pastor of the Baptist cause in Olney, Buckinghamshire. In the words of Ryland's son, Jonathan Edwards Ryland (1798–1866), they were "men of deep piety, and addicted to theological inquiries."[8]

---

6 Advertisement for "Global Jonathan Edwards Congress 2020" (https://www.jedcon2020.be/). On the impact of Edwards on Fuller, see Thomas J. Nettles, "The Influence of Jonathan Edwards on Andrew Fuller," *Eusebeia: The Bulletin of The Andrew Fuller Center for Baptist Studies* 9 (2008): 97–116; Chris Chun, "'Sense of the Heart': Jonathan Edwards' Legacy in the Writings of Andrew Fuller," *Eusebeia* 9 (2008): 117–134; and *idem*, *The Legacy of Jonathan Edwards in the Theology of Andrew Fuller*, Studies in the History of Christian Traditions, vol. 162 (Leiden; Boston, MA: Brill, 2012). In the words of David W. Bebbington, "Fuller more than anyone else ensured that the substance of Edwards' teaching exerted an enduring influence over his [Particular Baptist] denomination for most of the nineteenth century" ("The Reputation of Edwards Abroad" in Stephen J. Stein, ed., *The Cambridge Companion to Jonathan Edwards* [Cambridge: Cambridge University Press, 2007], 247).

7 The first edition appeared in 1785, and the second in 1801.

8 Ryland, "Fuller, Rev. Andrew," 324.

The critical role played by Fuller in this controversy with Hyper-Calvinism led to his engagement as an apologist in other vital areas of theological debate. In 1793, he issued an extensive refutation of the Socinianism of Joseph Priestley (1733–1804): *The Calvinistic and Socinian Systems Examined and Compared, as to Their Moral Tendency*. Due to the vigorous campaigning of Priestley, Socinianism, which denied the Trinity and the deity of Christ, had become the leading form of heterodoxy within English Dissent in the last quarter of the eighteenth century. Fuller's rebuttal of Socinianism well displayed the Christocentric nature of eighteenth-century evangelical thought. Fuller ably showed that the early church made the divine dignity and glory of Christ's person "their darling theme," for they "considered Christ as the all in all of their religion; and, as such, they loved him with their whole hearts."[9]

In 1800, Fuller published *The Gospel Its Own Witness*, the definitive eighteenth-century Baptist response to Deism, in particular that of the popularizer Thomas Paine (1737–1809). This work was one of the most popular of Fuller's books, going through three editions by 1802 and being reprinted a number of times in the next thirty years. William Wilberforce (1759–1833), who admired Fuller as a theologian and who once graphically described him as "the very picture of a blacksmith,"[10] considered it to be the most important of all of Fuller's writings.

9 Fuller, *Calvinistic and Socinian Systems Examined and Compared* in *Works of the Rev. Andrew Fuller*, 2:189, 192.

10 As quoted in "Art. I.—*The Life of William Wilberforce*. By his Sons, Robert Isaac Wilberforce ... and Samuel Wilberforce," *The British Critic, and Quarterly Theological Review* 24 (1838): 259; Robert Isaac Wilberforce and Samuel Wilberforce, *The Life of William Wilberforce* (London: John Murray, 1839), 3:388–389.

Fuller also wrote a major work against Sandemanianism. The Sandemanians, followers of Robert Sandeman (1718–1771), distinguished themselves from other eighteenth-century evangelicals by a predominantly intellectualist view of faith. They became known for their cardinal theological tenet that saving faith is "bare belief of the bare truth." In a seemingly genuine desire to exalt the utter freeness of God's salvation, Sandeman sought to remove any vestige of human reasoning, willing, or desiring in the matter of saving faith. In his response, *Strictures on Sandemanianism* (1810), Fuller drew heavily upon Jonathan Edwards' classic work of spirituality, *The Religious Affections* (1746), to make a couple of telling points. First, if faith does concern only the mind, then there would be no way to distinguish genuine Christianity from nominal Christianity. A nominal Christian mentally assents to the truths of Christianity, but those truths do not grip the heart or re-orient his or her affections. Then, knowledge of Christ is a distinct type of knowledge. Knowing him, for instance, involves far more than knowing certain things about him, such as the fact of his virgin birth or the details of his crucifixion. Rather, or in addition, it involves a desire for fellowship with him and a sweet delight in his presence.

FULLER AS A GLOBAL THEOLOGIAN AND LOCAL PASTOR

In addition to being a leading apologist, Fuller served as the secretary of the Baptist Missionary Society from its inception in October 1792 till his death. The work of the mission, which began with the sending of William Carey (1792–1834) to India, consumed an enormous amount of Fuller's time, as he regularly toured the country representing the mission and raising funds. On average, he was away from home three months of the year. Between 1798 and 1813, moreover, he made five lengthy trips to Scotland for the mission as well as undertaking journeys to Wales and Ireland (1804). He also carried on an extensive correspondence on the mission's behalf.

Fuller's commitment to the Baptist Missionary Society was rooted not only in his missionary theology but also in his deep friendship with Carey. Fuller later compared the sending of Carey to India as the lowering of him into a deep gold mine. And Fuller and his close friends, Sutcliff and Ryland, had pledged themselves to "hold the ropes" for as long as Carey lived.[11]

First and foremost, though, Fuller was a pastor, first at Soham and then at Kettering. And though he did not always succeed, he constantly sought to ensure that his many other responsibilities as a theologian and missionary secretary did not encroach upon those related to the pastorate.

During his thirty-three years at Kettering, from 1782 to 1815, the membership of the church more than doubled (from 88 to 174), and the number of "hearers" was often over a thousand, necessitating several additions to the church building. A letter and a sermon well display his pastoral heart. The letter is dated February 8, 1812, and was written to a wayward member of his flock. In it, Fuller lays bare his pastor's heart when he writes: "When a parent loses … a child[,] nothing but the recovery of that child can heal the wound. If he could have many other children, that would not do it … Thus it is with me towards you. Nothing but your return to God and the Church can heal the wound."[12]

11 As quoted in J. W. Morris, *Memoirs of the Life and Death of the Rev. Andrew Fuller* (London, 1816), 101.

12 As quoted in Gladys M. Barrett, *A Brief History of Fuller Church, Kettering* ([St. Albans, Herfordshire, c. 1946]), 10.

The sermon was a funeral sermon that Fuller had preached thirty years earlier, in April of 1792, when one of the deacons of the Kettering church, Beeby Wallis (1735–1792), died.[13] Beeby's great-grandfather, William Wallis, was the founding pastor of the Kettering church, while his grandfather, Thomas Wallis (d. 1726), was pastor when John Gill (1697–1771) was called to the ministry. Over the ten years that had elapsed since Fuller had moved to Kettering, Beeby, though nearly twenty years Fuller's senior, had formed a deep friendship with his pastor. In Fuller's words, he was "a steady, faithful, and judicious friend."[14]

Contrary to what was the practice in the Particular Baptist community, Fuller did not normally give a biographical sketch of the deceased in his funeral sermons. This occasion was different. Wallis had been such a force for good in the church that Fuller believed he had to say something about his life and character. Among the aspects of Wallis' character that Fuller highlighted was his humility:

> There are few men that have possessed a greater degree of genuine humility. It is often seen, where persons of affluence unite with a Christian community, they consider themselves as doing great honour to it, and expect great homage in return. But this every one that knew him can bear witness was not his spirit. It was not natural to him to assume the airs of a Diotrephes, or to avail himself of the

13 Andrew Fuller, *The Blessedness of the Dead Who Die in the Lord* in *Works of the Rev. Andrew Fuller*, 1:152–160. Fuller's memoir of Wallis runs from pages 157 to 160.

14 Fuller, *Blessedness of the Dead* in *Works of the Rev. Andrew Fuller*, 1:158, 157.

> influence which his circumstances and situation afforded him to lord it over God's heritage.[15]

It is patent that Wallis' humble leadership was, for Fuller, a model that he aspired to. As he had said earlier in the sermon as justification for speaking about the life of his deceased friend: "Perhaps no human writings have had a better effect than the lives of eminently holy men. When, therefore, any such characters appear among us, I think it is right to collect as much information respecting them as we can, that the remembrance of them may be of general use."[16]

John Ryland
(Wikimedia Commons)

15 Fuller, *Blessedness of the Dead* in *Works of the Rev. Andrew Fuller*, 1:159.

16 Fuller, *Blessedness of the Dead* in *Works of the Rev. Andrew Fuller*, 1:157–158.

THE EARLY YEARS AND EARLY MINISTRY OF JOHN RYLAND

In September 1753, Samuel Davies (1723–1761), a Presbyterian minister from Virginia, left his home for Great Britain on what would turn out to be an arduous, though highly successful, fundraising expedition for the then-fledgling College of New Jersey (later to be renamed Princeton University). He was gone for a total of eighteen months and met quite a number of key British evangelicals and churchmen, among them the leading Baptist theologian of that day, John Gill, whom he described as "the celebrated Baptist minister" and who had come to London in 1719. He paid a visit to Gill on January 30, 1754, and found him "a serious, grave little man." Gill was quite willing to lend his support to the College, but he told Davies not to expect much from the English Baptists as a whole: "In general," he said, the Baptists "were unhappily ignorant of the importance of learning."[17]

An exception to John Gill's censure of his fellow Baptists was his friend John Collett Ryland, who had a voracious appetite for learning. For much of his life, J. C. Ryland was pastor of College Lane Baptist Church, Northampton, and one of the leading Particular Baptist stalwarts of the eighteenth century.[18] He sought to stimulate a similar appetite for books and learning in his children, in particular

17 *The Reverend Samuel Davies Abroad: The Diary of a Journey to England and Scotland, 1753–55*, ed. George W. Pilcher (Urbana, IL; Chicago; London: University of Illinois Press, 1967), 65. The spelling of the quotes from Davies' diary have been modernized.

18 On John Collett Ryland, see Peter Naylor, "John Collett Ryland (1723–1792)" in Michael A.G. Haykin, ed., *British Particular Baptists, 1638–1910* (Springfield, MO: Particular Baptist Press, 1998), 1:184–201.

in his namesake, John Ryland, Jr.[19] For instance, in 1758 or so, the younger Ryland had been so fascinated by watching his father teach Hebrew to some boys that he apparently asked if he could learn Hebrew as well. So it was that before the age of six the young Ryland was able to read the Twenty-third Psalm in Hebrew! In fact, he remembered reading it to the notable evangelical author James Hervey (1714–1758), who was a close friend of his father.[20] The elder Ryland was, in the words of William Jay (1769–1853), the Congregationalist minister of Bath,

> much attached to many other preachers less systematically orthodox than himself; and laboured, as opportunity offered, with them. He was, indeed a lover of all good men; and, while many talked of candour, he exercised it.

---

19 The earliest memoir of Ryland is that found at the conclusion of Robert Hall, Jr., *A Sermon Occasioned by the Death of the Rev. John Ryland, D.D., Preached at the Baptist Meeting, Broadmead, Bristol, June 5, 1825* in *The Works of the Rev. Robert Hall, A.M.*, ed. Olinthus Gregory, 2nd ed. (London: Holdsworth and Ball, 1832), 1:389–414. A brief sketch by his son, Jonathan Edwards Ryland, appeared in the 1820s: "Memoir" in his ed., *Pastoral Memorials: Selected from the Manuscripts of the Late Revd. John Ryland, D.D. of Bristol* (London: B. J. Holdsworth, 1826), 1:1–56. Later in the nineteenth century, James Culross devoted a significant section of his *The Three Rylands: A Hundred Years of Various Christian Service* (London: Elliot Stock, 1897) to recounting the life and ministry of Ryland (pp. 69–91). Finally, Christopher W. Crocker has written recently an exhaustive biographical study: "The Life and Legacy of John Ryland Jr. (1753–1825): A Man of Considerable Usefulness—An Historical Biography" (Ph.D. dissertation, University of Bristol and Bristol Baptist College, 2018). For a concise examination of Ryland's theology, see L. G. Champion, "The Theology of John Ryland: Its Sources and Influences," *The Baptist Quarterly* 28 (1979–1980): 17–29.

20 John Ryland, "Autograph Reminiscences" (Ms. Z.f.31; Bristol College Library, Bristol College, Bristol), 52.

> Though he was a firm Baptist, he was no friend to bigotry or exclusiveness. [21]

The younger Ryland was a precocious child and genuinely loved study from an early age. He recalled that as a young child, he "was fond of reading, and generally preferred that employment to play."[22] In his father's diary for August 28, 1764, there is the following remarkable entry:

> John is now eleven years and seven months old; he has read Genesis in Hebrew five times through; he read through the Greek Testament before nine years old. He can read Horace and Virgil. He has read through Telemachus in French! He has read through Pope's Homer, in eleven volumes; read Dryden's Virgil, in three volumes. He has read Rollin's ancient history, ten volumes ... And he knows the Pagan mythology surprisingly.[23]

As H. Wheeler Robinson commented on this diary entry: "There is more than paternal pride in those words; there is the sense that he is giving to his boy that which he was once so eager to win for himself."[24] The elder Ryland's piety also influenced his son. Though at times quite eccentric, the father was an ardent lover of the Lord Jesus. "What a glory to be connected with all the infinite good in Christ,"

---

21 *The Autobiography of the Rev. William Jay*, ed. George Redford and John Angell James, 3rd ed. (London: Hamilton, Adams & Co., 1855), 293.

22 As quoted in Ryland, "Memoir" in his ed., *Pastoral Memorials*, 1:4.

23 As quoted in H. Wheeler Robinson, *The Life and Faith of the Baptists*, 2nd ed. (London: The Kingsgate Press, 1946), 64.

24 Robinson, *Life and Faith of the Baptists*, 64.

he wrote on one occasion in a small piece that enumerated reasons for prayer.[25] Thus, devotion and learning were interwoven early in the life of the younger Ryland.[26]

Ryland experienced conversion and baptism in 1767, and in March of 1771, the Northampton church formally recognized his gift for preaching. He was but eighteen years old. Many years later he could say that he had "had very few silent Sabbaths since."[27] In 1781, Ryland was invited by College Lane to become co-pastor with his father. When his father moved away to Enfield, then a market town near London, in 1786, Ryland became the sole pastor.

READING JONATHAN EDWARDS

During his early years of ministry, Ryland received much solid and judicious advice and encouragement from John Newton, the Anglican evangelical, a friendship that will be explored in the following chapter. Like Fuller, Ryland also read deeply in the writings of Jonathan Edwards.[28] Again, like Fuller, Edwards' writings, after the Scriptures, exerted the strongest theological influence on Ryland. As Ryland declared in a letter to his fellow Baptist Joseph Kinghorn (1766–1832):

25 John Collett Ryland, "Encouragements to Prayer" in John Rippon, ed., *The Baptist Annual Register, for 1798, 1799, 1800, and Part of 1801* (London, 1801), 366.

26 This interweaving of piety and theological reflection is well seen in a phrase that Ryland inserted in an ordination sermon by Samuel Spring (1746–1819), a New England preacher. At the point where Spring is describing the depth of the well of theology and observing that "fresh and pure water" can only be drawn out of this well by "hard study," Ryland has added "prayer &" just before "hard study" (Geoffrey F. Nuttall, "Some of John Ryland's Books," *The Baptist Quarterly* 33 [1989–1990]: 214).

27 Ryland, "Autograph Reminiscences," 44.

28 For references to Ryland's early acquaintance with the works of Jonathan Edwards, see Ryland, "Memoir," in his ed., *Pastoral Memorials*, 1:7, 15.

"Were I forced to part with all mere human compositions but three, Edwards' *Life of Brainerd*, his *Treatise on Religious Affections*, and [Joseph] Bellamy's *True Religion Delineated* ... would be the last I should let go."[29] And in a postscript to his funeral sermon for Fuller he stated: "If I knew I should be with ... Fuller tomorrow, instead of regretting that I had endeavoured to promote that religion delineated by Jonathan Edwards in his *Treatise on Religious Affections* and in his *Life of David Brainerd*, I would recommend his writings ... with the last effort I could make to guide a pen."[30]

The "religion delineated by Jonathan Edwards" was devoted to a scholarly and contemporary defense of Calvinistic convictions and to tracing the work of the Spirit in corporate revival and individual renewal. This twin commitment of Edwards' theological reflection provided both shape and substance for Ryland's own theology. Ryland deemed Edwards to be "one of the greatest and best of men" in his personal life, one whom Ryland esteemed as "the most skillful and successful opposer" of religious fanaticism, who, at the same time, was "one of the ablest defenders of the distinguishing doctrines of Revelation."[31]

What struck many who met Ryland for the first time was his humility. While one possible root of this virtue in Ryland's

---

29 As quoted in Martin Hood Wilkin, *Joseph Kinghorn of Norwich: A Memoir* (Norwich: Fletcher and Alexander, 1855), 183. For a discussion of Edwards' influence on Ryland, see L. G. Champion, "The Theology of John Ryland," 18–19. Joseph Bellamy (1719–1790) had been mentored by Edwards and served as a pastor in Bethlehem, Connecticut. *True Religion Delineated* was his most famous book.

30 John Ryland, *The Indwelling and Righteousness of Christ No Security against Corporeal Death, but the Source of Spiritual and Eternal Life* (London: W. Button & Son, 1815), 47.

31 John Ryland, *The Partiality and Unscriptural Direction of Socinian Zeal* (Bristol, 1801), 33.

life was a natural timidity and gentleness,[32] it was reverence for God and his holy character that matured it. In his funeral sermon for Ryland, Robert Hall, Jr., mentioned Ryland's "warm predilection" for the theology of Jonathan Edwards as being a major source for his love for God's holy character as it is in itself, and not for any benefits it bestows to the sinner. And it was this that gave him "the most elevated conceptions" of God and kept him far from "the slightest tendency to Antinomianism."[33]

Jonathan Edwards
(Wikimedia Commons)

32 According to his son, Jonathan Edwards Ryland (1798–1866), Ryland's "disposition was naturally retiring and unobtrusive" ("Memoir" in his ed., *Pastoral Memorials*, 1:18).

33 Hall, *Sermon Occasioned by the Death of the Rev. John Ryland*, 404–405.

TEACHING IN BRISTOL AND WRITING HYMNS

In 1793, Ryland moved to Bristol where, until his death in 1825, he was the pastor of Broadmead Church and the president of Bristol Baptist Academy. An outstanding Hebrew scholar and solid preacher, Ryland exercised a significant influence on the lives of the two hundred or so students who studied at Bristol during his time as president. The student body was never huge at any one time. In 1816, for example, there were twenty-two students studying at the school.[34] Yet, the majority of the graduates went on to become Baptist pastors and missionaries, imbued with Ryland's evangelical Calvinism and commitment to revival.

Over time, Ryland became one of the respected pillars of Particular Baptist life in England. On one occasion, when Robert Hall, his successor, was told something he regarded as incredible, Hall asked on whose authority the report was based. When he was told it was on that of Ryland, he replied, "Did Ryland say so, Sir? Then it is true, Sir; for I would as soon receive his testimony as the affidavit of seven archangels."[35]

Like his friend Newton, Ryland was a writer of hymns, of which a number had a wide circulation in nineteenth-century Baptist hymnals. John Julian, the editor of the well-known *A Dictionary of Hymnology,* pronounced them "plain and simple," lacking in "poetry and passion."[36] Elsie Houghton,

34 John Ryland, Letter to John Williams, April 5, 1816 (American Baptist Historical Society, Atlanta, GA).

35 William B. Sprague, *Visits to European Celebrities* (Boston: Gould and Lincoln, 1855), 63.

36 John Julian, *A Dictionary of Hymnology* (1907, New York: Dover Publications, Inc., 1957), 2:984. This judgment is echoed by Donald E. Demaray, *The Innovation of John Newton (1725–1807): Synergism of Word and Music in Eighteenth Century Evangelism* (Lewiston, NY; Queenston, ON: The Edwin Mellen Press, 1988), 209–210.

in her study of various hymn-writers, begged to differ. Referring to one hymn in particular, "O Lord, I Would Delight in Thee," she noted that the hymn seemed "to come straight from the experience of the writer's heart."[37] Houghton was right. As proof, consider the first stanza of this hymn of Ryland that is still being sung:

> O Lord, I would delight in Thee,
> And on thy care depend;
> To thee in every trouble flee,
> My best, my only Friend.[38]

Christ's friendship was precious to Ryland, since, as this hymn professed, it was marked by a deep care for Ryland's well-being. And as line 3 confessed, it was a friendship that possessed insuperable power to help Ryland whatever the trouble he might face. When we now come to look at Ryland's friendships with John Newton and then with Andrew Fuller, we need to bear in mind these convictions about the friendship of Christ. Christian friendships are a precious means of grace because they reflect, albeit imperfectly, the beautiful friendship of Jesus.

37 Elsie Houghton, *Christian Hymn-Writers* (Bryntirion, Bridgend, Mid Glamorgan: Evangelical Press of Wales, 1982), 168.

38 In John Rippon, *A Selection of Hymns*, 32nd ed. (London, [1832?]), Hymn #248.

Chapter 3

TO "TAKE SWEET COUNSEL TOGETHER"

The Friendship of John Newton and John Ryland

> "I heard by last post that my beloved friend Dr. [Isaac] Watts stood just on the verge of eternity. ... If he yet lives tell him my heart feels a flame of friendship for him which I am fully persuaded will burn forever."
>
> —Philip Doddridge, Letter (1748)

One of the most prominent features of the Evangelical Revival[1] in the eighteenth century was its genuinely catholic perspective when it came to ecclesiological issues. For instance, it was said of William Grimshaw (1708–1763), the influential evangelical curate of Haworth in Yorkshire, that he embraced Christians of all denominations, stating, "I love them and I will love them, and none shall make me do

1 In American parlance, this revival is known as the "Great Awakening."

otherwise: and my House shall always be open to them all."[2] Good evidence of Grimshaw's catholicity is to be found in his active support for Baptist causes throughout Yorkshire, despite the fact that a number of them had drawn some of their members from among Grimshaw's converts. Although such sheep-stealing did not sit well with Grimshaw, he was able to joke about it, saying, "The worst of it is, that so many of my chickens turn ducks!"[3]

Historian Geoffrey F. Nuttall is surely right when he says of the evangelical leaders in general that "whether Arminian or Calvinist in doctrine, whether Dissenters or clergy of the Establishment, ... these men and many others, were working together—in no all embracing organizations, but in close bonds of friendship, correspondence and inter-visitation."[4] These "close bonds of friendship, correspondence and inter-visitation" are possibly nowhere better seen than in the friendship between the Anglican John Newton and the Baptist John Ryland, Jr.[5]

---

2 Frank Baker, *William Grimshaw, 1708–1763* (London: The Epworth Press, 1963), 245.

3 Baker, *William Grimshaw*, 243. For Grimshaw's relationship with Baptists, see Michael A.G. Haykin, "'Dissent Warmed Its Hands at Grimshaw's Fire.' William Grimshaw of Haworth and the Baptists of Yorkshire," *Perichoresis* 7, no. 1 (2009): 23–37.

4 Geoffrey F. Nuttall, *Howel Harris, 1714–1773: The Last Enthusiast* (Cardiff: University of Wales Press, 1965), 29.

5 A major source for studying the friendship between Newton and Ryland is a collection of letters from the former to the latter, now housed in the Bristol Baptist College Library, Bristol. This correspondence covers the period from January 22, 1774, to April 23, 1803. For a published edition of the correspondence, see Grant Gordon, ed., *Wise Counsel: John Newton's Letters to John Ryland, Jr.* (Edinburgh; Carlisle, PA: Banner of Truth Trust, 2009). L. G. Champion examines some aspects of these letters in "The Letters of John Newton to John Ryland," *The Baptist Quarterly* 27 (1977–1978): 157–163.

A stained-glass portrait of John Newton in St. Peter and St. Paul Church, Olney, Buckinghamshire (Photograph, Michael A.G. Haykin).

BEING JOHN NEWTON

John Newton is certainly one of the most colorful figures of the eighteenth-century Evangelical Revival. In his early childhood, Newton received a religious upbringing from his mother, Elizabeth. Newton remembered her as "a pious, experienced Christian,"[6] from whom he learned the rudiments of

6 *The Life and Spirituality of John Newton*, introd. Bruce Hindmarsh (Vancouver, BC: Regent College Publishing, 2003), 17. This work contains Newton's *Authentic Narrative of Some Remarkable and Interesting Particulars in the Life of* —— (1764),

piety that he was never completely able to erase despite his later dissolute years.[7] Four years after the death of his mother in 1732, Newton's father, also called John Newton (d. 1750), a captain in the Merchant Marine, took his son to sea with him. Over the next twelve years as a sailor, Newton sought to rid himself entirely of his mother's godly instruction. He embraced the viewpoint of a free-thinking Deist, came to be adept in ridiculing Christianity, and liberally peppered his speech with coarse language and blasphemies. In his words:

> My whole life, when awake, was a course of most horrid impiety and profaneness. I know not that I have since met with so daring a blasphemer. Not content with common oaths and imprecations, I daily invented new ones.[8]

During a fearsome storm on the Atlantic on March 21, 1748, however, when it seemed impossible that the ship on which he was a sailor would not founder, Newton was shocked to hear a cry to God for mercy issue from his own mouth, his first real prayer in many years. The ship did not

---

which recounts the story of Newton's early years and conversion. For a study of this work, see David Lyle Jeffrey, *People of the Book: Christian Identity and Literary Culture* (Grand Rapids, MI; Cambridge, UK: Eerdmans, 1996), 288–300.

7 D. Bruce Hindmarsh, *John Newton and the English Evangelical Tradition between the Conversions of Wesley and Wilberforce* (Oxford: Clarendon Press, 1996), 52–54. For other biographies of Newton, see especially Josiah Bull, *John Newton of Olney and St. Mary Woolnoth* (1868, Edinburgh; Carlisle, PA: Banner of Truth Trust, 1998); Bernard Martin, *John Newton: A Biography* (Melbourne; London; Toronto, ON: William Heinemann, 1950); and Jonathan Aitken, *John Newton: From Disgrace to Amazing Grace* (Wheaton, IL: Crossway Books, 2007).

8 Bull, *John Newton of Olney*, 23.

sink, and Newton later remarked, "About this time, I began to know that there is a God who hears and answers prayer."[9]

Newton was set now on the path of seeking to find the true God, though it was not until 1754 that he was firmly within the fold of evangelical Christianity. A providential meeting with a naval captain by the name of Alexander Clunie (d. 1770) on the Caribbean island of St. Kitts was critical in Newton's spiritual growth. According to Newton's later recollection:

> [Clunie] not only improved my understanding, but inflamed my heart. He encouraged me to open my mouth in social prayer. He put me upon an attempt to make my profession more public, and to venture to speak for God. From him, or, rather, from the Lord, by his means, I received an increase of knowledge, my conceptions became clearer and more evangelical, and I was delivered from a fear which had long troubled me—the fear of relapsing into my former apostasy. But now I began to understand the security of the covenant of grace, and to expect to be preserved, not by my own power and holiness, but by the mighty power and promise of God through faith in an unchangeable Saviour.[10]

A few years after his conversion, he became a tide-surveyor in Liverpool. It was there that he first met evangelical leaders such as George Whitefield (1714–1770) and Grimshaw, who, with others, encouraged him

9 Bull, *John Newton of Olney*, 27.
10 Bull, *John Newton of Olney*, 58.

to think of entering the ministry. After meeting with some disappointments, Newton was ordained to the Anglican ministry in 1764 and became the curate-in-charge of the church of St. Peter and St. Paul in the market town of Olney, Buckinghamshire. Newton ministered at Olney until 1780, when he accepted an offer to move to St. Mary Woolnoth, London, where he pastored till his death in 1807. In both the Church of St. Peter and St. Paul in Olney and St. Mary Woolnoth, Newton regularly preached to large crowds, though compared to other preachers of his day, his preaching was not remarkable.[11] His close friend and fellow hymn-writer William Cowper (1731–1800) once described his preaching as simply "plain and neat."[12]

Newton did excel as a hymn-writer, and it is as such that he is mainly remembered today for what has become an iconic song of North American culture, "Amazing Grace," originally entitled "Faith's Review and Expectation."[13] However, his key contribution to eighteenth-century evangelicalism was in the realm of spiritual mentoring and guidance, especially

---

11 Ernest Gordon Rupp, *Religion in England 1688—1791*, Oxford History of the Christian Church (Oxford: Clarendon Press, 1986), 482; Tony Baker, *1807–2007: John Newton and the Twenty-First Century*, St. Antholin's Lectureship Charity Lecture (London: Latimer Trust, 2007), 15–18.

12 Martin, *John Newton*, 231–232.

13 Newton's hymns can be found in *Olney Hymns, in Three Books* (London, 1779). A facsimile edition of this work was published by The Cowper and Newton Museum, Olney, Buckinghamshire, in 1979. It bears noting that the hymnal was not entirely Newton's work. Of the 348 hymns in this volume, William Cowper wrote 67. For studies of the hymns, see Robin A. Leaver, "Olney Hymns 1779: 1. The book and its origins," *Churchman* 93 (1979): 327–342; *idem*, "Olney Hymns 1779: 2. The hymns and their use," *Churchman* 94 (1980): 58–66; *idem*, "Olney Hymns: A documentary footnote," *Churchman* 97 (1983): 244–245; J. R. Watson, *The English Hymn: A Critical and Historical Study* (Oxford: Clarendon Press, 1997), 282–299; and William E. Phipps, *Amazing Grace in John Newton: Slave-Ship Captain, Hymn-writer, and Abolitionist* (Macon, GA: Mercer University Press, 2001), 115–158.

through the medium of the letter. As Anglican historian G. R. Balleine once expressed it, Newton was "the great spiritual director of souls through the post."[14] Newton's use of written correspondence as a conduit of friendship and spiritual formation was facilitated, first, by the increased efficiency of the post office and mail delivery in Newton's day. The development of a writing style that was simpler and less convoluted than the baroque prolixity of seventeenth-century theologians like John Owen (1616–1683) also made spiritual letters like those of Newton a joy to read.[15]

NEWTON'S FRIENDSHIPS

Consider his letters to the Scottish Congregationalist minister John Campbell (1766–1840), who began corresponding with Newton in 1789, when Newton was sixty-four years of age and Campbell a young man of twenty-three. Over the course of their correspondence, Newton built a close friendship with the young Scotsman, which enabled him to speak plainly to Campbell. In June of 1792, for instance, he urged Campbell never to write off Socinians (that is, Unitarians) as beyond the grace of God: "Grace has long and strong arms and I think it more becoming a Christian to be unwilling to give anyone up, while living."[16] Again, despite his urging the evangelical politician William Wilberforce (1759–1833) to continue to serve God in the realm of

14 G. R. Balleine, *A History of the Evangelical Party in the Church of England* (London: Longmans, Green, and Co., 1908), 107.

15 Baker, *John Newton and the Twenty-First Century*, 22–23.

16 John Newton, Letter to John Campbell, June 2, 1792, in *Letters and Conversations: John Newton's Restored Letters to John Campbell*, ed. Sean Richardson (1811, self-published, 2020), 17.

politics and his subsequent mentoring of the politician, Newton told Campbell that he was still convinced that "it is well both for ministers and private Christians to have as little to do with politics as possible." Campbell agreed with Newton and suggested that politics was a pit. "Your idea of a pit in the path," Newton told the Scotsman, "pleases me. I am afraid it is a pit that will swallow up the life and spirit, if not the very form of the religion of many professors."[17]

In his letters, Newton also often recommended books that he was convinced would help his young friend. In August of 1794, Newton told Campbell that he considered Andrew Fuller's *The Calvinistic and Socinian Systems Examined and Compared*, which had appeared the previous year,[18] as "the most complete unanswerable refutation of the Socinian scheme" that he had read. "The great learned doctors dodged Dr. Priestley about in Greek and Latin to little purpose: it was reserved to Mr. Fuller, a plain, unlettered Baptist, who was never so much as at a Grammar School, to cut off this great Goliath's head."[19] And sprinkled throughout the correspondence are pithy sayings of sage Christian wisdom, such as: "The heart is like gunpowder, which lies quiet if fire be kept from it; but a single spark, in the Lord's time, is sufficient to set it in a blaze."[20]

---

17 John Newton, Letter to John Campbell, January 23, 1793, in *Letters and Conversations*, ed. Richardson, 28.

18 See above, page 46.

19 John Newton, Letter to John Campbell, August 1, 1794, in *Letters and Conversations*, ed. Richardson, 61–62, altered. This published version omits the clause "a plain, unlettered Baptist, who was never so much as at a Grammar School," which can be found in the original manuscript. I am indebted to Dr. Grant Gordon for this information in an email of July 8, 2021.

20 John Newton, Letter to John Campbell, September 2, 1795, in *Letters and Conversations*, ed. Richardson, 107.

John Campbell
(from John Campbell, Travels in South Africa: Undertaken at the Request of the Missionary Society [Andover, MA: Flagg and Gould, 1816], frontispiece)

Or consider Newton's friendship with John Ryland, which dated from 1768, a few years after the former had become the curate at the parish church in Olney.[21] "We began," Newton wrote to Ryland in 1795, "when you were a lad and I a curate and we have gone on till you are grown into a doctor and I am dignified with the title of rector."[22] Though belonging to different generations, both men deeply valued their friendship. Near the end of his life, Newton could write to his friend: "If, as is possible, this should be my last letter to you, keep it as a memorial of the love I bear you, and of

21 John Ryland, "Remarks on the Quarterly Review, for April 1824, Relative to the Memoirs of Scott and Newton," in Jonathan Edwards Ryland, ed., *Pastoral Memorials: Selected from the Manuscripts of the Late Revd. John Ryland, D.D. of Bristol* (London: B. J. Holdsworth, 1828), 2:346.

22 John Newton, Letter to John Ryland, July 28, 1795, in Gordon, ed., *Wise Counsel*, 317.

my thankful remembrance of past times, when being within a few miles, we could see each other often, take sweet counsel together, and go to the house of our God in company."[23]

And the year before Ryland died, he recalled, "Mr. Newton invited me to visit him at Olney in 1768; and from thence to his death, I always esteemed him, and Mr. Hall of Arnsby ... as my wisest and most faithful counsellors, in all difficulties.[24] The truth of this assertion by Ryland is readily seen even by a cursory examination of the letters he received from Newton. Over the years, he consulted Newton about a variety of personal matters, ranging from prospective marriages (Ryland married twice) to his decision to leave his pastorate in Northampton for the one in Bristol.

MANAGING WITH JOHN COLLETT RYLAND

One of the matters in which Newton's friendship was a great help had to do with Ryland's father. The elder Ryland was a very candid man, often incorrigibly impetuous, and sometimes very unwise in his choice of words, all of which gave his son much anguish of heart. It was Ryland, for example, who, at a meeting of the ministers of the Northamptonshire Association in 1785, asked William Carey (1761–1834), who had just become the minister of the Baptist cause in the village of Moulton, Northamptonshire, to propose a subject

23 John Newton, Letter to John Ryland, January 16, 1801, in Gordon, ed., *Wise Counsel*, 379.

24 Ryland, "Remarks on the Quarterly Review," in Ryland, ed., *Pastoral Memorials*, 2:346. Robert Hall, Sr., of Arnesby, Leicestershire, was a Baptist pastor. On his life and ministry see Graham W. Hughes, "Robert Hall of Arnesby: 1728–1791," *The Baptist Quarterly* 10 (1940–1941): 444–447 and Michael A.G. Haykin, "Robert Hall, Sr., 1728–1791," in his and Terry Wolever, eds., *The British Particular Baptists* (Springfield, MO: Particular Baptist Press, 2019), 5:54–63.

for discussion for the ministerial meeting. Carey suggested a subject on which he had been long ruminating: "Whether the command given to the apostles to teach all nations was not binding on all succeeding ministers, to the end of the world, seeing that the accompanying promise was of equal extent."

Carey's question grew out of his reflection on Matthew 28:18–20. The promise Carey had in mind is clearly that given by the Lord Jesus in verse 20, and the command that in verse 19a. If, Carey reasoned, Christ's promise of his presence is for all time (v. 20), then what of his command (v. 19a)?

There is considerable debate about the older Ryland's response. According to John Webster Morris (1763–1836), pastor of Clipston Baptist Church in Northamptonshire, who was actually present, Ryland responded thus to Carey:

> You are a miserable enthusiast for asking such a question. Certainly nothing can be done before another Pentecost, when an effusion of miraculous gifts, including the gift of tongues, will give effect to the commission of Christ as at first. What, Sir! Can you preach in Arabic, in Persic, in Hindustani, in Bengali, that you think it your duty to send the gospel to the heathens?

John C. Marshman, the son of Carey's respected coworker in India, Joshua Marshman (1768–1837), reported a more abrupt retort by the elder Ryland: "Young man, sit down. When God pleases to convert the heathen, he will do it without your aid or mine!" John Ryland, Jr., on the other hand, strongly asserted that his father never uttered such sentiments.[25]

---

25 For discussion of this incident and the words attributed to the elder Ryland, see especially John Ryland, Jr., *The Work of Faith, the Labour of Love, and the Patience of*

Though the younger Ryland denied the historicity of this particular outburst of his father, which most students of this era acknowledge to have taken place, other similar incidents could not be denied. As William Jay observed, the elder Ryland's speech was marked by "bold sayings and occasional sallies of temperament," and though a man whose "excellencies ... more than balanced his defects," he was, all in all, "a peculiar character, and had many things about him *outré* and *bizarre*, as the French would call them."[26] On one occasion, Jay recorded, Ryland had preached about angels and had mentioned their presence at Christian worship. The congregational singing after his sermon, however, was so bad that Ryland halted the singing midstream and told the congregation, "I do not wonder the angels of God do not wrench your necks off."[27] On another occasion, Jay witnessed Ryland's impassioned response to the slave trade:

Hope, Illustrated; in the Life and Death of the Rev. Andrew Fuller, 2nd ed. (London: Button & Son, 1818), 112, note; S. Pearce Carey, *William Carey*, 8th ed. (London: The Carey Press, 1934), 54; F. Deaville Walker, *William Carey: Missionary Pioneer and Statesman* (Chicago, IL: Moody Press, 1925), 54–55; Iain H. Murray, *The Puritan Hope. A Study in Revival and the Interpretation of Prophecy* (Edinburgh: The Banner of Truth, 1971), 139 and 280, n.14; *idem*, "William Carey: Climbing the Rainbow," *The Banner of Truth* 349 (October 1992): 18–21; Ruth Tucker, "William Carey: Father of Modern Missions" in John D. Woodbridge, ed., *Great Leaders of the Christian Church* (Chicago, IL: Moody Press, 1988), 308; Brian Stanley, *The History of the Baptist Missionary Society 1792–1992* (Edinburgh: T & T Clark, 1992), 6–7; and Michael A.G. Haykin, *One Heart and One Soul: John Sutcliff of Olney, His Friends and His Times* (Darlington, Co. Durham: Evangelical Press, 1994), 193–196.

26 *The Autobiography of the Rev. William Jay*, ed. George Redford and John Angell James, 3rd ed. (London: Hamilton, Adams & Co., 1855), 286.

27 *Autobiography of the Rev. William Jay*, ed. Redford and James, 293.

> One morning I was reading to him some of the reported miseries and cruelties of the middle passage; among others, of a captain who had a fine female slave in his cabin, but, when her infant cried, he snatched him up, and flung him out into the sea; still requiring the wretched creature to remain, as the gratifier of his vile passions. At the recital of this Mr. Ryland seemed frantic, and to lose his usual self-control. He was agitated, and paced up and down the room, "O God, preserve me! O God, preserve me!" and then, unable to contain any longer, burst forth into a dreadful imprecation, which I dare not repeat. It shocked me, and I am far from justifying it; and yet, had the reader been present to witness the excitement and the struggle, he would hardly have been severe in condemning him.[28]

When the younger Ryland thus asked Newton for advice about what he should do with regard to his father's eccentricities, Newton's advice was especially helpful. In a letter dated March 26, 1791, Newton advised Ryland:

> I have always admired [Ryland Sr.]: his love to the truth and to souls; his zeal and benevolence have appeared to me exemplary. His eccentricities and failures have likewise been great, but I think they were constitutional chiefly. He will leave them behind him, with the mortal part, and perhaps the blemishes may be more visible, and his excellencies more clouded the longer he lives.[29]

28 *Autobiography of the Rev. William Jay*, ed. Redford and James, 290–291.

29 John Newton, Letter to John Ryland, March 26, 1791, in Gordon, ed., *Wise Counsel*, 241–242.

Again, the following year, on January 31, 1792, when Ryland, Jr., was still disturbed by some of his father's behavior at times—this time it appears he had publicly criticized his own son—Newton told him:

> Poor man, I love and pity him. I am persuaded his most conspicuous failings are strictly constitutional. He acts according to the impetus of his spirits, is hurried away, and I believe he cannot help it. ... I would no more write against such a man, though he is not *my* father, than I would employ my right hand to wound my left.[30]

John Collett Ryland
(Courtesy of Grant Gordon)

30 John Newton, Letter to John Ryland, January 31, 1792, in Gordon, ed., *Wise Counsel*, 255–256.

RESPONDING TO WILLIAM HUNTINGTON

Another example of Newton's wise counsel to Ryland is found in relation to Ryland's controversy with the Antinomian author William Huntington (1745–1813), who helped foment a dissension in Ryland's church. A popular London preacher whose preaching was a curious and heady mix of bombast, Tory politics, and rancorous denunciation of any who dared to criticize him,[31] Huntington played a significant role in the propagation of Antinomian principles in the late eighteenth century. Though he was not a Baptist, numerous Baptists imbibed his argument that the moral law should not be considered as a pattern for the Christian life and that any like the two Rylands who did regard it as such were simply nothing more than "Pharisees" and guilty of "undervaluing Christ's imputed righteousness."[32]

In the early 1790s, Huntington penned a number of vicious pamphlet attacks on the elder Ryland and Caleb Evans (1737–1791), who was the president of Bristol Baptist Academy at the time. A Mr. Adams from Ryland's congregation

31 For contrasting perspectives on Huntington, see George M. Ella, *William Huntington: Pastor of Providence* (Darlington, Co. Durham, England: Evangelical Press, 1994) and Robert W. Oliver, *History of the English Calvinistic Baptists 1771–1892: From John Gill to C. H. Spurgeon* (Edinburgh; Carlisle, PA: The Banner of Truth Trust, 2006), 119–145. Huntington went so far as to imply that any who strenuously opposed him would be struck dead by God. See John Ryland, *Serious Remarks on the Different Representations of Evangelical Doctrine by the Professed Friends of the Gospel* (Bristol, 1817), 2:39–41.

32 Robert W. Oliver, "The Emergence of a Strict and Particular Baptist Community among the English Calvinistic Baptists, 1770–1850" (Ph.D. thesis, London Bible College, 1986), 130; John Ryland, *The Practical Influence of Evangelical Religion* (London, 1819), 38. Oliver's thesis is essentially the same as that of his *History of the English Calvinistic Baptists: From John Gill to C. H. Spurgeon* (Edinburgh; Carlisle, PA: The Banner of Truth Trust, 2006), though not all of the material in the thesis appears in the book, and vice versa.

sided with Huntington against his pastors and invited him to Northampton to preach. Huntington even had the effrontery to ask Ryland if he could speak from his pulpit! When Adams was eventually disfellowshipped, Huntington wrote an eighty-four-page booklet against the younger Ryland, and the latter's congregation ended up losing close to two dozen members—it decreased from 206 in 1782 to 183 in 1792[33]—due to the controversy.

Ryland asked Newton what he should do. Should he respond to Huntingdon's pamphlet? Newton's advice was sage and sound. On January 25, 1792, he wrote to Ryland:

> [W]hen you speak, as not being fully determined whether to answer this doughty pamphlet, or not, I am a little alarmed. And as it seems there are some who advise it, I am willing to throw my mite into the opposite scale. But I think if you regard your own character you will pity and pray for the writer in silence. If a chimney-sweeper insulted you in the street, would you demean yourself so low as to fight him? Let him alone, and he will expose himself more effectually than you can expose him. And his performance will soon die and be forgotten, unless you keep the memory of it alive, by an answer. I believe scarcely any thing has [contributed] so much to perpetuate disputes and dissensions in the professing church, as the ambition of having the last word.

33 College Lane Church Book (Northamptonshire Record Office, Northampton, England), 134.

> His fan is in his hand [cf. Matt. 3:12]. He has sent a fan to Northampton, to rid you of some chaff. Why should this grieve or displease you? If any simple people whose hearts are better than their heads are drawn away at first, give them time, and the Lord will show them their folly, and deliver them. He knows them that are his.[34]

The following week, Newton gave further advice about the matter:

> The embers at Northampton will soon go out, if you do not keep them alive, and blow them up. I have such a love for you and for peace, that, if money would prevent it, I would give something out of my pocket rather than see you degrade yourself, and perplex your people, by answering a performance which deserves no other treatment than silent contempt.[35]

Ryland followed his friend's advice to the letter and must have thanked God that he had such a faithful friend and wise counselor. Moreover, having known the value of having an older, trusted friend like Newton when he was young would have served Ryland in good stead when he came to befriend students under his care at Bristol Baptist Academy.

---

34 John Newton, Letter to John Ryland, January 25, 1792, in Gordon, ed., *Wise Counsel*, 251–252.

35 John Newton, Letter to John Ryland, January 31, 1792, in Gordon, ed., *Wise Counsel*, 258.

Chapter 4

"WE MUST … BE TOGETHER AS MUCH AS POSSIBLE"

The Friendship of Andrew Fuller and Thomas Steevens

> "I am a dull flint, you must strike me against a steel to produce fire."
>
> —Andrew Fuller, Letter to John Fountain (1799)

In the fall of 1799, William Wales Horne (1773–1826), the minister of the Baptist cause in Great Yarmouth, East Norfolk, gave two addresses that were later published together as a pamphlet entitled *The Faith of the Gospel Vindicated* (1800). Part of the pamphlet attacked the idea that "Evangelical faith … [is] the duty of the unconverted." As Horne went on to argue, "If faith is the work of the Spirit, and at the same time the duty of the creature, it consequently follows, that it is the duty of a man dead in sin, to give himself the Spirit of God! A sentiment equally as absurd as presumptuous! and to be detested by all sincere advocates for the glory of free grace!"[1] In other words, Horne denied the free offer of the gospel to all and sundry.[2]

Not surprisingly, when this pamphlet fell into the hands of that day's most ardent defender of the affirmation that faith is indeed the duty of all to whom the gospel comes, namely, Andrew Fuller, he fired off a small piece that has been transmitted under the title "Remarks on Two Sermons by W. W. Horne of Yarmouth."[3] Among other things, Fuller was distressed that Horne had used the pulpit to launch an attack on those, like him, who held to the free offer of the gospel. As he said:

> It is not by converting the pulpit into a stage of strife, nor by availing ourselves of the silence which decency imposes upon an audience to pour forth personal invective, that truth is promoted. … It is by reading, by calm and serious reflection, by humble prayer, and by a free and friendly communication of our thoughts to one another in private conversation, that truth makes progress.[4]

---

1 William Wales Horne, *The Faith of the Gospel Vindicated: Being the Substance of Two Sermons, Delivered Extempore at the Baptist Meeting, Great Yarmouth, Oct. 27, 1799* (Yarmouth, 1800), 33.

2 Horne, *Faith of the Gospel Vindicated*, 26–27. Elsewhere, Horne claimed to be a defender of "repentance toward God, and faith toward our Lord Jesus Christ, as covenant blessings, the free gifts of Jehovah, and of the operation of the Holy Spirit in the souls of the redeemed, against the duty faith men, or Semi-arminians" (*Biblical Criticisms and Illustrations of Experimental Godliness, The Solutions to Critical Questions in Theology* [London: W. Day, 1825], vi).

3 Andrew Fuller, "Remarks on Two Sermons by W. W. Horne of Yarmouth" in *Works of the Rev. Andrew Fuller*, 3:578–585. Horne subsequently replied to Fuller with his *A Scriptural Defence of the Truth, as it is in Jesus* (Nottingham: J. Plumbe, 1801) and sarcastically referred to him as "a great master in Baptist Israel."

4 Fuller, "Remarks on Two Sermons by W. W. Horne of Yarmouth" in *Works of the Rev. Andrew Fuller*, 3:582.

In these occasional remarks, Fuller revealed a fundamental aspect of his thinking about right and wrong ways to promote biblical truth. Truth was to be promoted through what historically have been called the means of grace. Fuller mentioned four in this text—reflective reading, meditation on what has been read, prayer, and personal conversations—all of which were part of Fuller's own way of appropriating and disseminating truth and piety.[5] The final one—"free and friendly communication of our thoughts to one another in private conversation"—is especially noteworthy, for this means of grace is the very thing that this book has been emphasizing.[6] As we have seen, Fuller was blessed to be part of a close-knit circle of friends. He thus knew from personal experience how vital it was to sit down with such men and talk through issues.

"SUCH LIVES AS BRAINERD AND EDWARDS"

An excellent window on the way that Fuller and his friends sat down and talked to one another face to face, as it were, is found in an entry in John Ryland's diary for January 21, 1788:

5 See the references to Fuller in Michael A.G. Haykin, "'Draw Nigh unto My Soul': English Baptist Piety and the Means of Grace in the Seventeenth and Eighteenth Centuries," *The Southern Baptist Journal of Theology* 10, no. 4 (Winter 2006): 54–73. See also Nathan A. Finn, "Andrew Fuller's Edwardsean Spirituality" in G. Stephen Weaver and Ian Hugh Clary, eds., *The Pure Flame of Devotion: The History of Christian Spirituality. Essays in Honour of Michael A.G. Haykin* (Kitchener, ON: Joshua Press, 2013), 383–404.

6 See also the argument of Joanne J. Jung, *The Lost Discipline of Conversation. Surprising Lessons in Spiritual Formation Drawn from the English Puritans* (Grand Rapids, MI: Zondervan, 2018).

> Brethren Fuller, Sutcliff, Carey, and I, kept this day as a private fast in my study: read the Epistles to Timothy and Titus; Booth's Charge to Hopkins; Blackerby's Life, in Gillies; and Rogers of Dedham's Sixty Memorials for a Godly Life: and each prayed twice—Carey with singular enlargement and pungency. Our chief design was to implore a revival of the power of godliness in our own souls, in our churches, and in the church at large.[7]

Three specific works beyond the apostle Paul's pastoral epistles are mentioned here. First, there was the classic ministerial charge by Abraham Booth (1734–1806) to Thomas Hopkins (1759–1787), known as *Pastoral Cautions* (1785).[8] Booth filled the pulpit for nearly forty years of one of the most prestigious London churches, Little Prescot Street Baptist Church, in what was then a wealthy area of London, home to merchants and professionals. As a theologian, he stood high in the regard of Fuller and his circle of friends, and indeed, in the esteem of their entire denomination. In 1808, two years after Booth had died, Fuller publicly praised Booth as "the first counsellor of our denomination."[9] Earlier, while Booth was still living, Benjamin Beddome (1718–1795), one of the most significant Baptist hymn-writers of the era, exclaimed, "Oh, that Abraham Booth's God may be my God."[10] The other

7 As quoted in Jonathan Edwards Ryland, "Memoir," in his *Pastoral Memorials: Selected from the Manuscripts of the Late Rev^d. John Ryland, D.D. of Bristol* (London: B. J. Holdsworth, 1826), 1:17, note *.

8 See *The Works of Abraham Booth*, ed. Michael A.G. Haykin with Alison E. Haykin (Springfield, MO: Particular Baptist Press, 2006), 1:57–84.

9 As quoted in Ernest A. Payne, "Abraham Booth, 1734–1806," *The Baptist Quarterly* 26 (1975–1976): 28.

10 As quoted in John Rippon, *A Short Memoir of the Rev. Abraham Booth* in James

works that Fuller and his circle of friends read were both Puritan items: the life of Richard Blackerby (1574–1648), which was published in John Gillies' *Historical Collections Relating to Remarkable Periods of the Success of the Gospel, and Eminent Instruments Employed in Promoting It* (1754), and *Sixty Memorials of a Godly Life,* frequently assigned to John Rogers of Dedham (d. 1636), a fiery Puritan preacher.[11]

As has been already noted, the works of Jonathan Edwards were also being deeply read and discussed by this "band of brothers."[12] To take but one example, in the summer of 1793, Fuller wrote to Thomas Steevens, the pastor of Colchester Baptist Church, Essex, from 1774 until his death, that when he read about "such lives as Brainerd and Edwards, I am utterly ashamed of my own."[13] Fuller is referring here to the life of the American missionary David Brainerd (1718–1747), which had been written by Edwards shortly after the former's death, and Samuel Hopkins' (1721–1803) *The Life and Character of the Late Reverend, Learned, and Pious Mr. Jonathan Edwards* (1764), which Fuller possessed in a 1785 Glasgow edition.[14] Obviously, he expected Steevens to be familiar with both biographies.

Dore, *A Sermon, Occasioned by the Death of The Rev. Abraham Booth, Preached in Little Prescot Street, Goodman's Fields...: and A Short Memoir of the Deceased, Incorporated with The Address Delivered at His Interment...by John Rippon* (London, 1806), 85, note *.

11 For a brief review of Rogers' character and ministry, see Michael A.G. Haykin, "A Boanerges and a Barnabas," *Tabletalk* 36, no. 3 (March 2012): 32–33.

12 See above, pp. 54–56.

13 Andrew Fuller, Letter to Thomas Steevens, July 8, 1793, in "Extracts from the Late Rev. A. Fuller's Correspondence with the Late Rev. Mr. Steevens, of Colchester," *The Baptist Magazine* 8 (1816): 494.

14 For Fuller's possession of these books, see "Books in Fuller's Library, 1798" in Michael D. McMullen and Timothy D. Whelan, eds., *The Diary of Andrew Fuller, 1780–1801,* The Complete Works of Andrew Fuller, vol. 1 (Berlin; Boston: Walter de Gruyter, 2016), 221.

In the midst of setting aside an entire day to pray, they also took time to read both the Bible and good Christian literature and then to discuss the content of what they read. By speaking to one another about what they read, they sought to inflame their hearts and strengthen their wills in God's service. Thus, reflection on and discussion of both Scripture and Christian literature deeply shaped and informed the lives of Fuller and his friends.

"I ADMIRE THE SPIRIT OF THE AUTHOR"

When Fuller was unable to meet his friends face to face, he used the medium of the letter to convey the "free and friendly communication of [his] thoughts."[15] With this in view, the remainder of this chapter will consider a slice of his correspondence with the Colchester pastor just mentioned, Thomas Steevens.[16]

Steevens was born in Northamptonshire, where his parents had sat under the powerful ministry of the Congregationalist Philip Doddridge (1702–1751). Another leading influence on him in his early years was the somewhat eccentric John Ryland, Sr., whom we met in the previous chapter. Steevens himself was baptized as a believer in July of 1771 by John Macgowan (1726–1780) at Devonshire Square Baptist Church in London, and two years later called by this church to a preaching ministry.[17]

15 Fuller, "Remarks on Two Sermons by W. W. Horne of Yarmouth" in *Works of the Rev. Andrew Fuller*, 3:582.

16 For his life, see the anonymous "Memoir of the Rev. Thomas Steevens," *The Baptist Magazine* 9 (1817): 81–88.

17 "Memoir of the Rev. Thomas Steevens," 83; Henry Spyvee, *Colchester Baptist Church—The First 300 Years, 1689–1989* (Colchester: Colchester Baptist Church 1989), 31. Spyvee calls the London pastor "Joseph Macgowan." The anonymous memoir from *The Baptist Magazine* places Steevens' baptism in 1772, though

Thomas Steevens
(from The Baptist Magazine 9 [1817]: 80)

Steevens' first and only pastoral charge was over the Eld Lane congregation of Baptists in Colchester, where he began to preach in January of 1774 and to which he was formally called as pastor in May of that year. Despite the fact that the congregation was characterized by a contentious spirit from time to time, Steevens had a highly successful ministry.[18]

Timothy Whelan places it in 1771: "Biographical Index of Dissenters, 1700–1860" (https://sites.google.com/a/georgiasouthern.edu/tim-whelan/dissenting-studies/biographical-index-dissenters-1700-1860; accessed August 5, 2018). On Macgowan, see Charlotte Fell-Smith, revised by J. H. Y. Briggs, "Macgowan, John (1726–1780)," *Oxford Dictionary of National Biography* (Oxford University Press, 2004; online ed. [https://doi-org.proxy1.lib.uwo.ca/10.1093/ref:odnb/17516; accessed August 5, 2018]).

18 Spyvee, *Colchester Baptist Church*, 32; Janet Cooper and W. R. Powell, "Protestant Nonconformity" in Janet Cooper, ed., *A History of the County of Essex. Volume IX:*

Some 169 people were baptized during his pastorate and came into the membership of the congregation, which had to double the size of the church building to accommodate all of the congregants.[19] Steevens also played a key role in the formation of the Essex Baptist Association at Coggeshall in 1796,[20] and he was an ardent advocate of the cause of foreign missions, which endeared him to Fuller.

The first extant contact of the Fuller circle of friends with Thomas Steevens appears to be a letter that Steevens wrote to John Sutcliff on November 10, 1785, and which Sutcliff received three weeks later. Steevens had read Fuller's *The Gospel of Christ Worthy of All Acceptation*, which had appeared earlier in 1785, and was convinced that he and Fuller shared much theologically:

> You wish to know my thoughts of that gentleman's [i.e., Fuller's] publication—I will be perfectly free, however much I may prove myself precipitate & even ignorant in what I wrote before.—I admire the spirit of the author—it appears plain I think that his alone wish is to propagate

---

The Borough of Colchester (Oxford: The Institute of Historical Research by Oxford University Press, 1994), 340–341. In 1785, Steevens told John Sutcliff that some of his congregation were complaining that he was "wishing them to be more holy than God requires"! See Thomas Steevens, Letter to John Sutcliff, November 10, 1785, in Timothy Whelan, transcribed and ed., *Baptist Autographs in the John Rylands University Library of Manchester, 1741–1845* (Macon, GA: Mercer University Press, 2009), 48.

19 "Memoir of the Rev. Thomas Steevens," 85.

20 Steevens preached his sermon *The Knowledge of God Increased, and His Church Enlarged* (London, 1796) at the founding of the Association. He also spoke the following year at the Association's first anniversary, which was held in the Congregationalist Church in Coggeshall. See George Frederick Beaumont, *A History of Coggeshall, in Essex* (London: Marshall Brothers; Coggeshall: Edwin Potter, 1890), 149.

> truth—I admire the perspicuity of his manner which conveys at once his meaning to the mind—Nor can I find anything to say against, but much to say for the sentiment. I was rather averse to it before, either because I did not understand it, or because it was wrongly stated by others—the last I think was the chief reason; for I now recollect, that for seven years past & more I have been coming over to his mind tho' I did not know, that I had any partners—thinking upon that text with a view to the pulpit "ye will not come to me that you may have life" [John 5:40] led me into a quite (for me) new train of thought upon man's inability & I found and said it lies in his will. ... It appears to me that M^r^ F[uller] deserves the thanks of all the lovers of simple truth ...[21]

Fuller's book was designed to affirm both divine sovereignty in the salvation of sinners and human responsibility to respond to the gospel proclamation.[22] And although Steevens, in the early stages of his ministry in Colchester, would have found fault with Fuller's theology, by the time that he read

---

21 Steevens, Letter to Sutcliff, November 10, 1785, in Whelan, transcribed and ed., *Baptist Autographs*, 47. For the entire letter, see pp. 46–48. Spelling modernized.

22 See the discussion by Keith S. Grant, *Andrew Fuller and the Evangelical Renewal of Pastoral Theology*, Studies in Baptist History and Thought, vol. 36 (Milton Keynes, UK: Paternoster, 2013), 45–49; Peter J. Morden, "Andrew Fuller and the Birth of 'Fullerism,'" *Baptist Quarterly* 46 (2015): 139–152; and Michael A.G. Haykin, "A Historical and Biblical Root of the Globalization of Christianity: The Fullerism of Andrew Fuller's *The Gospel Worthy of All Acceptation*," *Puritan Reformed Journal* 8, no. 1 (January 2016): 165–176.

For Fuller's confidence in God's sovereignty in the conversion of sinners, see his Letter to Thomas Steevens, April 14, 1795, in "Extracts from the Late Rev. A. Fuller's Correspondence with the Late Rev. Mr. Steevens, of Colchester," 495: "Men's hearts there [in India], are the same as here; nothing short of an Almighty arm, will pull down the strong holds of error and superstition."

The Gospel of Christ Worthy of All Acceptation he realized that his own theological development paralleled that of Fuller. It is noteworthy that Steevens used the phrase "I will be perfectly free," which is an expression that best characterizes frank and open discussion between friends.

Yet there were many known to Steevens who were firm in their refusal to see Fuller's theology as anything but a variant of Arminianism. As Steevens went on in this letter to Sutcliff:

> [I]t pleases me, that some very sensible Independents hereabout have the Book [of Fuller] and esteem it—But my Baptist Brethren will not receive it & some of them already deem me an Arminian for only attempting to explain to them the meaning of the phrases moral & natural inability—I have had some warm, I don't mean angry, disputes upon the subject.[23]

The counties of Suffolk and Norfolk, to the immediate north of Steevens' church in Colchester, Essex, contained a good number of High Calvinist congregations, that is, churches that generally regarded the free offer of the gospel to all and sundry as a dangerous error. Witness William Wales Horne, the critic of Fuller with whom this chapter began.[24]

23 Steevens, Letter to Sutcliff, November 10, 1785, in Whelan, transcribed and ed., *Baptist Autographs*, 47. Spelling modernized. "Independents" are Congregationalists.

24 See also *A Testimony in Favour of the Principles Maintained by the Suffolk and Norfolk Association of Particular Baptist Churches, on the Doctrines of Grace* (London: W. Button, 1807), in which Fuller and his theology were repeatedly and extensively attacked by name (3, 9, 13–14, 20–23). Fuller was criticized for erecting "a stately fabric of creature-holiness and mere morality" (9) and his argumentation likened to that characteristic of Arminian authors (14).

In fact, the term "Fullerism" may well have originated in this locale. The Norfolk Baptist pastor Job Hupton (1762–1849), for example, employed this term as early as 1803 in a pamphlet to denote specifically the concept, erroneous in his mind, that it is "the duty of all who hear the gospel to believe it." In this pithy phrase, Hupton accurately caught an essential aspect of Fuller's thinking, though the same cannot be said for his further critique of Fuller's theology as that of a "buffoon" who regarded all "who cannot swallow his sophisms, or subscribe to his creed, as if they were not worthy to black his shoes."[25]

Fuller's response to Hupton's pamphlet was an 1804 book review in which he commented:

> To call the principles opposed in this piece [by Hupton] *Fullerism* ... shows but little acquaintance with things. If the doctrine which Mr. Fuller has defended contained anything new, or different from what has been taught by all our divines, except a few in the last century, there might have been some colour for giving it a new name. But it does not: and therefore it might as well be called Calvinism, Owenism or Bunyanism, as Fullerism.[26]

Fuller was confident that his theology had much deeper roots in the Reformed tradition than his own reflections and theological struggles with High Calvinism.

25 Job Hupton, "Preface" to his *A Blow Struck at the Root of Fullerism* (London: L. J. Higham, [1803]) (http://www.mountzionpbc.org/Duty%20Faith/Job_Hupton_Fullerism.pdf; accessed August 6, 2018).

26 As quoted in J. W. Morris, *Memoirs of the Life and Writings of the Rev. Andrew Fuller*, rev. ed. (London: Wightman and Cramp, 1826), 238–239.

"WE WISH TO DO SOMETHING MORE THAN PRAY"

Fuller's first extant letter to Steevens comes from the spring of 1793, when Fuller sought to acquaint his fellow pastor with details regarding the progress of the Baptist Missionary Society (BMS), which Fuller and his friends had founded in 1792.[27] Fuller informed Steevens about the way that the Society had been led to appoint a surgeon named John Thomas (1757–1801) to accompany William Carey as a missionary to India.[28] During an earlier voyage to India in 1786, Thomas had become friends with Charles Grant (1746–1823), an Anglican evangelical who was on the Board of Trade of the powerful East India Company and who was based in Calcutta. Grant had helped Thomas start a missionary enterprise in Bengal, where Thomas began to learn Bengali and to translate the Scriptures into that tongue; he also made some headway in learning Sanskrit. He was deeply moved by the wretchedness, both spiritual and material, of many of the Indian people and longed to alleviate it.

For a variety of reasons, not the least of which was a significant financial indebtedness and Thomas' mercurial temper, by 1790 the friendship between Thomas and Grant had soured to the point that Thomas had had to return to England in the early months of 1792 to secure a new source of funding to undergird his missionary work in Bengal. He also hoped to find, if at all possible, a like-minded companion

27 Andrew Fuller, Letter to Thomas Steevens, [1793], in "Extracts from the Late Rev. A. Fuller's Correspondence with the Late Rev. Mr. Steevens, of Colchester," 452–453.

28 On Thomas, see Arthur C. Chute, *John Thomas, First Baptist Missionary to Bengal. 1757–1801* (Halifax, NS: Baptist Book and Tract Society, 1893) and Michael Whitfield, "Dr. John Thomas: The First Baptist Missionary to Bengal," *Baptist Quarterly* 46 (2015): 153–165.

for the work in India. Almost as soon as the ship had made landfall in England on July 8, Thomas got in touch with the London pastors Samuel Stennett (1727–1795) and Abraham Booth. He made known to them his desire with regard to a mission to India, and it was Booth who put Thomas into contact with Carey and Fuller. Booth told Fuller that he considered Thomas "a suitable person" to send with Carey.[29]

William Carey (This rendition of a famous portrait of Carey is owned by McMaster Divinity College, used by permission)

29 Fuller, Letter to Steevens, [1793], in "Extracts from the Late Rev. A. Fuller's Correspondence," 452. For further detail regarding Fuller's decision to send Thomas with Carey, see Michael A.G. Haykin, *One Heart and One Soul: John Sutcliff of Olney, His Friends and His Times* (Darlington, Co. Durham, England: Evangelical Press, 1994), 225–227.

Steevens did not know Carey personally, but Fuller told him that he was "a noble creature, ready at learning languages; open, generous, and upright; ardent—of sound principles—a disinterested soul, and a heart that comprehends the welfare of a world."[30] Here, in these few phrases, Fuller described his close friend Carey to a tee: his ability to learn languages, his transparent goodness, and his ardency for truth and for the salvation of the lost. These were essential qualities that had drawn Fuller to become Carey's close friend. Fuller went on to note that "there were difficulties" in the path of the mission, but Carey was "formed on purpose to surmount difficulty."[31] Of course, key among these difficulties would have been the reluctance of Carey's wife, Dorothy Plackett Carey (1756–1807), to accompany her husband, though Fuller did not mention this specifically to Steevens.[32]

This mission to India, Fuller hastened to add, was not a matter of a few months' planning. It grew out of close to a decade of prayer: "We have not gone about this business in a hurry; we have been praying by monthly prayer-meetings for it these eight or nine years, and now we wish to do something more than pray."[33] This is a reference to what is known as the Prayer Call of 1784, by which Fuller and his friends had encouraged the Northamptonshire Baptist Association to gather on a monthly basis to pray for

30 Fuller, Letter to Steevens, [1793], in "Extracts from the Late Rev. A. Fuller's Correspondence," 453.

31 Fuller, Letter to Steevens, [1793], in "Extracts from the Late Rev. A. Fuller's Correspondence," 453.

32 See the very balanced account of Dorothy's life by James Beck, *Dorothy Carey: The Tragic and Untold Story of Mrs. William Carey* (1992, Eugene, OR: Wipf and Stock, 2000).

33 Fuller, Letter to Steevens, [1793], in "Extracts from the Late Rev. A. Fuller's Correspondence," 453.

revival in the British Isles and also that there would be a spread of the gospel "to the most distant parts of the habitable globe."[34]

Fuller further noted that he and his friends in the Northamptonshire Association "have solemnly bound ourselves to God, and one another" to engage in supporting this mission "by individual subscriptions, and congregational collections." Fuller communicated these details with the hope that Steevens and his Colchester church could help financially. "We exert ourselves to the utmost," Fuller commented, but at the same time "we rely upon God, trusting he will open the hearts of our brethren in every quarter of the kingdom, to assist in this good work." This combination of radical commitment and total trust in divine sovereignty is typically Fuller. Finally, the way that Fuller closed this initial letter to the Essex pastor augured a deepening friendship: "I am, Dear Sir, your affectionate brother in our dear Lord."[35]

"SWEET AND SAVOURY PLEASANTRY"

Regretfully, none of Steevens' letters to Fuller appear to be extant. But he evidently replied to Fuller's first letter before Fuller wrote a second time on March 26, 1793. In this second letter, Fuller was thrilled to tell Steevens that £800 had already been raised, though none of it had come from

34 [John Sutcliff,] "The Prayer Call of 1784" in John Ryland, Jr., *The Nature, Evidences, and Advantages of Humility* (Circular Letter of the Northamptonshire Association, 1784), 12. For a detailed discussion of this call to prayer and its historical context, see Haykin, *One Heart and One Soul*, 153–171.

35 Fuller, Letter to Steevens, [1793], in "Extracts from the Late Rev. A. Fuller's Correspondence," 453.

the wealthy Baptist congregations in London. There, far too many had followed the advice of Samuel Stennett, who had urged extreme caution. "The mission," Fuller quoted him as saying, "will come to nothing from this cause—people may contribute ... for once in a fit of zeal, but how is it to be [continually] supported?"[36] Fuller's response to Stennett's skepticism was to declare that his trust was not in human support and resources at all, but in God. As he told Steevens:

> For my part, I believe in God, and have not much doubt but that a matter, begun as this was, will meet his approbation: and that he who has inclined the hearts of our brethren hitherto so much beyond our expectations, will go on to incline their hearts "not to lose the things which they have wrought" [2 John 1:8]. I confess I feel sanguine in my hopes, but they are fixed in God.[37]

Fuller's hope was not misplaced: by the early nineteenth century, the BMS was regularly receiving £3,000 or more a year.[38]

In his closing remarks, Fuller included Zenas Trivett (d. 1831), the pastor of the Baptist cause in Langham, Essex, from 1778 to 1819:

---

36 Andrew Fuller, Letter to Thomas Steevens, March 26, 1793, in "Extracts from the Late Rev. A. Fuller's Correspondence," 453.

37 Fuller, Letter to Steevens, March 26, 1793, in "Extracts from the Late Rev. A. Fuller's Correspondence," 453.

38 This may be readily seen by consulting the subscription lists contained in the *Periodical Accounts* issued by the BMS during the first dozen years of the nineteenth century.

> My Christian love to Mr. Trivet, or any others you may think proper. A thousand thanks to you and him for your exertions. ... If I were within a day's ride of you any time, I should be tempted to come and see you. ... Grace be with you, so prays your affectionate, A. Fuller. Brother Ryland unites in love.[39]

Although Fuller had not yet met Steevens face to face, the latter's warm advocacy of the missionary cause dear to Fuller's heart had quickened the latter's desire to meet him as well as the expressions of love he declared.[40]

The way in which the churches that supported the BMS were bound together in love was the keynote of Fuller's next letter to Steevens, which was dated May 18, 1793:

39 Fuller, Letter to Steevens, March 26, 1793, in "Extracts from the Late Rev. A. Fuller's Correspondence," 454. Zenas Trivett was the youngest son of Edward Trivett (1712–1792), the pastor of a thriving Baptist work in Worstead, Norfolk. Ten years after Trivett retired from Langham, the congregation numbered around 450, the bulk of which had been added during Trivett's ministry. See Joseph Ivimey, *A History of the English Baptists* (London: Isaac Taylor Hinton and Holdsworth & Ball, 1830), 4:125, 524; "Obituary: Rev. Zenas Trivett," *The Baptist Magazine*, 23 (1831): 537–538; Maurice F. Hewett, "Early Days at Worstead," *The Baptist Quarterly* 11 (1942–1945): 168–170. Proof that it was indeed Zenas Trivett is found in Andrew Fuller, Letter to Thomas Steevens, October 5, 1793, in "Extracts from the Late Rev. A. Fuller's Correspondence," 494, where Fuller mentioned his visit to Langham. Trivett also preached Steevens' funeral sermon ("Memoir of the Rev. Thomas Steevens," 87).

Sadly, there is no mention in the minute books of the Langham church of its early support of the BMS (J. E. Compton, "Colchester and the Missionary Movement," *The Baptist Quarterly* 11 [1942–1945]: 55). The Baptist chapel in Langham closed around 1939. See Christopher Stell, *An Inventory of Nonconformist Chapels and Meeting-Houses in Eastern England* (Swindon: English Heritage, 2002), 58.

40 For love as a key element in Fuller's understanding of pastoral practice, see Paul A. Sanchez, *The Spirituality of Love in Andrew Fuller's Ordination Sermons* (Louisville, KY: The Andrew Fuller Center for Baptist Studies, 2018).

My dear brother,

I cannot but bless God for this business, in many points of view. One is, it introduces me to a more intimate acquaintance with my brethren, whom, as I know, I dearly love. The names of Fawcett, and Crabtree, and Pearce, and Birt, and Steadman, and Steevens, and many more, are hereby embalmed in my remembrance for ever.

I knew the opposition made to "Andrew Fuller," in S[uffolk] and N[orfolk], and though you may think me fond of fighting, I am too much a lover of peace and quietness, to embroil myself in unnecessary disputes, and which, in that case, I suppose, would be like a bear with his nose in a wasp's nest.

… O my dear brother, it would do your heart good to see the love to Christ, and the souls of men, discovered in many parts of the country, in readily contributing to this business. Good old Mr. Crabtree, of Bradford, in Yorkshire, upwards of seventy, could not sleep for joy: he laboured night and day, went to the vicar and curate, who cheerfully gave him a guinea each; obtained in the whole upwards of £40 and a great deal of respect from the neighbourhood into the account. "My heart has been so much in this work," says the venerable man, "that it has almost been too much for my poor old body." "Blessed be God," says dear Mr. Fawcett, of Brearly-hall, near Halifax, "that I have lived to see so much love to Christ. I account it one of the greatest blessings of my life, to have assisted in so glorious and disinterested an undertaking." Birt, of Plymouth-dock; Steadman, of Broughton, in Hampshire, and many more, write all in the same strain. I feel an exquisite satisfaction that we have made the attempt: the issue is in his hands, whose cause it is.[41]

41 Andrew Fuller, Letter to Thomas Steevens, May 18, 1793, in "Extracts from the Late Rev. A. Fuller's Correspondence," 454.

The larger English Particular Baptist community to which both Fuller and Steevens belonged did not have a national framework until the nineteenth century, but as this letter indicates, support for and engagement in overseas missions helped to unify and bring Baptists into loving contact and work together throughout England. In addition to Steevens, five other Baptist leaders are mentioned here: John Fawcett (1740–1817) and William Crabtree (1720–1811), both pastoring in the West Riding of Yorkshire, Samuel Pearce (1766–1799) of Birmingham, Isaiah Birt (1758–1837) of Plymouth, and William Steadman (1764–1837) from Broughton, Hampshire.[42] The cords of mission that

42 John Fawcett (1740–1817) was an important influence for revival among the Yorkshire Baptists. On his life and ministry, see [John Fawcett, Jr.], *An Account of the Life, Ministry, and Writings of the Late Rev. John Fawcett D.D.* (London: Baldwin, Cradock, and Joy; Halifax: P. K. Holden, 1818); Ian Sellers, "Other Times, Other Ministries: John Fawcett and Alexander McLaren," *The Baptist Quarterly* 32 (1986–1987): 181–199; Michael A.G. Haykin, *"Blest be the tie that binds": Remembering John Fawcett: His Times, His Life, His Hymn* (Louisville, KY: Andrew Fuller Center for Baptist Studies, 2018).

William Crabtree (1720–1811) was pastor of the Baptist cause in Bradford, Yorkshire for fifty years. For his life and ministry, see Isaac Mann, *Memoirs of the Late Rev. Wm. Crabtree* (London: Button and Son, 1815).

Samuel Pearce was one of Fuller's closest friends. Fuller wrote his memoir after Pearce's early death in 1799, which became the most printed work from Fuller's pen in the nineteenth century. See Andrew Fuller, *Memoirs of the Late Rev. Samuel Pearce, A. M.* (Clipstone: J. W. Morris, 1800). For Pearce's piety, see Michael A.G. Haykin, *Joy Unspeakable and Full of Glory: The Piety of Samuel and Sarah Pearce* (Kitchener, ON: Joshua Press, 2012).

Isaiah Birt (1758–1837) pastored Baptist churches at Plymouth Dock and in Birmingham. See John Birt, "Memoir of the Late Rev. Isaiah Birt," *The Baptist Magazine* 30 (1838): 54–59, 107–116, 197–203.

William Steadman (1764–1837) pastored at Broughton, Hampshire, from 1791 to 1798. He assisted Birt at Plymouth Dock from 1798 to 1805, when he moved to Bradford. In the north he not only pastored, but also became the president of Horton Academy. See Thomas Steadman, *Memoir of the Rev. William Steadman, D.D.* (London: Thomas Ward and Co., 1838); Sharon James, "William Steadman (1764–1837) in Michael A.G. Haykin, ed., *The British Particular Baptists,*

bound Fuller to these men were not simply that, as Fuller emphasized. The mission was a vehicle that deepened Fuller's love for these men.

The Baptist Church in Eld Lane, Colchester (Wikimedia Commons)

Thomas Steevens once wrote of the people of this church in a hymn entitled "A Pastor's Wish":

Brethren and sisters bought with blood,
Partakers of the grace of God;
In whom religion's proof I view,
I wish to die, and live with you. …

With you, when life and death are o'er,
In heav'n Jehovah to adore
Casting our crowns at Jesus' feet,
Will make your Pastor's wish complete.

1638–1910 (Springfield, MO: Particular Baptist Press, 2000), 2:162–181.

Though ev'ry saint will have his part
In the warm friendship of my heart,
'Tis you, I pray, may then be found,
My joy, my glory, and my crown.[43]

Commenting on the opposition to his theology in Norfolk and Suffolk, which has already been noted above, Fuller emphasized that he was not at heart a lover of theological conflict, nor, as he put it vividly, did he have any desire to be like "a bear with his nose in a wasp's nest." And yet, Fuller spent a good portion of his life as an author embroiled in theological battles.[44]

First, there was the conflict with the High Calvinists, as has been related. Then, in the early 1790s, it was the growing threat of anti-Trinitarian Socinianism, the leading heterodox movement of the late eighteenth century, which dominated Fuller's thinking as he wrote an extensive work against its principal apostle, namely, Joseph Priestley (1733–1804).[45] In this letter to Steevens, Fuller referred to both of these theological conflicts:

43 Thomas Steevens, "A Pastor's Wish," Hymn #348, in James Upton, ed., *Hymns Designed as a New Supplement to Dr. Watts' Psalms and Hymns* (London, 1815).

44 As Fuller wrote to Carey on April 18, 1799: "I sometimes say Woe is me, for I am born to be a man of strife! Here are Arminians, Socinians, & final Restitutionists always provoking me to write. I seem like a sort of pugilist, who having made a little noise in the world draws upon himself every one that fancies he can master him." ("The Letters of Andrew Fuller—Copied from Various Sources," typescript ms., transcribed Joyce A. Booth, and collected Ernest A. Payne [Angus Library, Regent's Park College, University of Oxford]).

45 For this work, see Andrew Fuller, *The Calvinistic and Socinian Systems Examined and Compared, as to their Moral Tendency* in *Works of the Rev. Andrew Fuller*, 2:108–233. Edward Hitchin (d. 1774), minister of White's Row Independent Chapel, Spitalifields, wrote to Priestley's cousin, also named Joseph Priestley, in 1768 that the famous author's "pride is likely to burst him __ He is the Solomon of our Infidels" (*Samuel Gedge Catalogue XXIII* [Norwich, UK: Samuel Gedge Ltd., n.d.], 63).

> I feel a sacred satisfaction in the principles I have endeavoured to state and define. They are such in the main that I can venture upon for eternity. Those which I have attempted to refute still appear to me, and that with abundantly increasing evidence, to be the bane of the churches. They unnerve the Christian for spiritual activity. By what I have read and written in the Socinian controversy, I feel more attached to the great doctrines of Christ's deity and atonement, together with those of salvation by grace alone, from first to last. These truths are not merely the objects of my faith, but the ground of all my hope, and administer what is superior to my daily bread. Excuse this egotism.[46]

From Fuller's perspective, the principles of High Calvinism undermined the spirituality of Christian congregations, for they discouraged mission and evangelism and provided ground for Antinomianism. Refuting Socinianism, on the other hand, had deepened Fuller's commitment to Christ's deity and his substitutionary atonement, as well as the Reformation assertion that salvation is "by grace alone, from first to last."[47] The final sentence of this passage is fascinating. Even in a face-to-face encounter with a man whom he counted as a friend, Fuller evidently found it distasteful to be going on about himself. Of course, since a true friendship is a face-to-face engagement, something has to be said about one's inner

46 Fuller, Letter to Steevens, May 18, 1793, in "Extracts from the Late Rev. A. Fuller's Correspondence," 455.

47 Fuller later told Steevens that he hoped his work against Priestley would "demolish the Socinian scheme" (Letter to Steevens, April 14, 1795, in "Extracts from the Late Rev. A. Fuller's Correspondence," 495). For another reference to Socinianism in these letters to Steevens, see Andrew Fuller, Letter to Thomas Steevens, June 19, 1795, in "Extracts from the Late Rev. A. Fuller's Correspondence," 496.

world and thoughts. But a true friendship has its main orientation away from oneself and towards the friend.

In addition to these remarks about the missionary society and Fuller's writing projects, Fuller also commented on Steevens' letters: "Art thou nervous, brother? Thy letters include so much sweet and savory pleasantry, that they are almost enough to cure a man that is so. I had almost said, 'Physician, heal thyself' [Luke 4:23]."[48] Since none of Steevens' letters to Fuller are extant, it cannot be known what exactly drew forth this praise of Steevens' prose as giving Fuller "sweet and savory" enjoyment. Fuller's concluding remarks once again mentioned Zenas Trivett and his desire for fellowship with him and Steevens: "Remember me affectionately to Mr. Trivet, when you see him, our hearty thanks await him for his exertions. If I should come a little before harvest, we must all three be together as much as possible."

"THINKING OF THOSE WHOM I LOVE"

Fuller was able to visit Steevens in Colchester and Trivett at Langham that September, a visit that he told Steevens on October 5 that he would "always remember ... with pleasure."[49] Fuller went on to comment about his desire to be closer geographically to Steevens: "I wish I could oftener enjoy your company, but Providence has ordered it otherwise, and, no doubt, wisely ordered it. If we do good, as salt in the earth, it must be by being spread."[50] Fuller had obviously found in

48 Fuller, Letter to Steevens, May 18, 1793, in "Extracts from the Late Rev. A. Fuller's Correspondence," 454.

49 Fuller, Letter to Steevens, October 5, 1793, in "Extracts from the Late Rev. A. Fuller's Correspondence," 494.

50 Fuller, Letter to Steevens, October 5, 1793, in "Extracts from the Late Rev. A. Fuller's Correspondence," 494.

Steevens a kindred spirit, but Fuller's evangelical passion to be "doing good" led him to recognize the wisdom of God's providence in placing them where they lived.[51]

Fuller then mentioned a meeting of the pastors of the Northamptonshire Association, which happened on a regular basis and was crucial in the formation of Fuller's appreciation of the necessity of spiritual conversation and friendship. It had been "pleasant and profitable," especially since Samuel Pearce and Benjamin Francis (1735–1799) of Horsley, Gloucestershire, had been present and preached. "They are excellent men of God," Fuller observed.[52] After a couple of remarks on the state of his physical health, Fuller commented on his struggle with depression, and here also Fuller found a kinship with Steevens: "I suppose I am little akin to you, though cheerful in company, frequently dejected alone; with this difference, that mine is not the hypochondriac affection (so, I think, your complaints are called), but a kind of constitutional gloom."[53]

In his recent biographical study of Fuller, Peter J. Morden has persuasively shown that from 1782 to 1792

---

51 In a diary entry for July 18, 1794, Fuller commented about Acts 10:38: "It seemed a lovely thing which is said of Christ, 'He went about doing good'!" (McMullen and Whelan, ed., *Diary of Andrew Fuller*, 188).

52 Fuller, Letter to Steevens, October 5, 1793, in "Extracts from the Late Rev. A. Fuller's Correspondence," 494. For Francis, see Thomas Flint, "A Brief Narrative of the Life and Death of the Rev. Benjamin Francis, A.M.," annexed to John Ryland, Jr., *The Presence of Christ the Source of Eternal Bliss. A Funeral Discourse, ... Occasioned by the Death of the Rev. Benjamin Francis, A.M.* (Bristol, 1800), 33–76; Geoffrey F. Nuttall, "Questions and Answers: An Eighteenth-Century Correspondence," *The Baptist Quarterly* 27 (1977–1978): 83–90; Michael A.G. Haykin, "Benjamin Francis (1734–1799)" in his ed., *The British Particular Baptists, 1638–1910* (Springfield, MO: Particular Baptist Press, 2000), 2:16–29.

53 Fuller, Letter to Steevens, October 5, 1793, in "Extracts from the Late Rev. A. Fuller's Correspondence," 494.

Fuller wrestled with both spiritual and clinical depression. His involvement in the founding of the Baptist Missionary Society eventually enabled him to emerge from this spiritual winter when he was, to employ a title from the Puritan Thomas Goodwin (1600–1679), "a child of light walking in darkness."[54] As this letter to Steevens reveals, however, he was still wrestling with depression a year after the founding of the BMS.

In this struggle with depression Fuller found help in a hymn written by John Fawcett that Fuller sang or read during this period. As he told Steevens:

> I never had any talent for composing hymns, yet I read the hymns of others with much pleasure. How often have I, of late, wept, in reading, or singing over the 324th hymn of Rippon's Selection, written by my dear friend Fawcett.—Also the 254th of the same selection, and composed by the same hand. Do read and sing it over, and think of me, and others. I have been ready to shed tears of joy while I have been singing it, in thinking of those whom I love, not only at and about Kettering, but in Yorkshire, in Birmingham, in Bristol, in Hampshire, in Cambridgeshire, in London, in Essex, and (I hope by this time, nearly) in Indostan!
>
> You have indulged yourself in many a solitary hour in composing hymns.—You have volumes of them.—Probably some of the notes of your plaintive soul might sound

54 Peter J. Morden, *The Life and Thought of Andrew Fuller (1754–1815)*, Studies in Evangelical History and Thought (Milton Keynes, England: Paternoster, 2015), 103–109.

> in unison with my feelings.—Would it be too much to ask you to send me a volume of them, by Mr. Perkins? I will peruse them about a year, and then return them.[55]

"Rippon's Selection" was, of course, John Rippon's (1751–1836) justly popular *A Selection of Hymns, From the Best Authors*, which was first published by this Baptist author in 1787 and over the course of Rippon's lifetime went through thirty-one editions.[56] Fuller's citation of it here illustrates the way it became de facto "*the* Baptist collection" of hymns for Baptist congregations in the British Isles and America.[57]

By 1793, four editions of the hymnal had appeared, and all four listed John Fawcett's "Thus far my God hath led me on" as hymn number 324. Its first three stanzas are not at all uplifting, but, as Fuller had experienced, they are all too frequently true in the lives of God's saints:

> Thus far my God hath led me on,
> And made his Truth and Mercy known;
> My Hopes and Fears alternate rise,
> And Comforts mingle with my Sighs.
>
> Thro' this wide Wilderness I roam,
> Far distant from my blissful Home;

---

55 Fuller, Letter to Steevens, October 5, 1793, in "Extracts from the Late Rev. A. Fuller's Correspondence," 494–495.

56 Ken R. Manley, *'Redeeming Love Proclaim': John Rippon and the Baptists*, Studies in Baptist History and Thought, vol. 12 (Carlisle, Cumbria; Waynesboro, GA: Paternoster Press, 2004), 82–138, 295–297.

57 Manley, *'Redeeming Love Proclaim'*, 136.

Lord, let thy Presence be my Stay,
And guard me in this dangerous Way.

Temptations every where annoy,
And Sins and Snares my Peace destroy;
My earthly Joys are from me torn,
And oft an absent God I mourn.[58]

The other hymn, numbered 254 by Rippon, is Fawcett's most well-known hymnic piece, "Blest be the tie that binds."[59] Given its theme of the blessing of Christian friendship in both this world and eternity, it is not surprising that as Fuller sang or read it, he was moved to "shed tears of joy." The following stanzas brought joy and love flooding into his heart as he thought of Christian friends in the North of England, its West Country, its capital, and East Anglia:

Blest be the tie that binds
Our hearts in Christian love;
The fellowship of kindred minds
Is like to that above.

Before our Father's throne
We pour our ardent pray'rs;
Our fears, our hopes, our aims are one,
Our comforts and our cares.

---

58 In John Rippon, *A Selection of Hymns*, 32nd ed. (London, [1832?]), Hymn #324.

59 For a discussion of the context and theology of this hymn, see Haykin, *"Blest be the tie that binds,"* 23–29.

We share our mutual woes;
Our mutual burdens bear;
And often for each other flows
The sympathizing tear.[60]

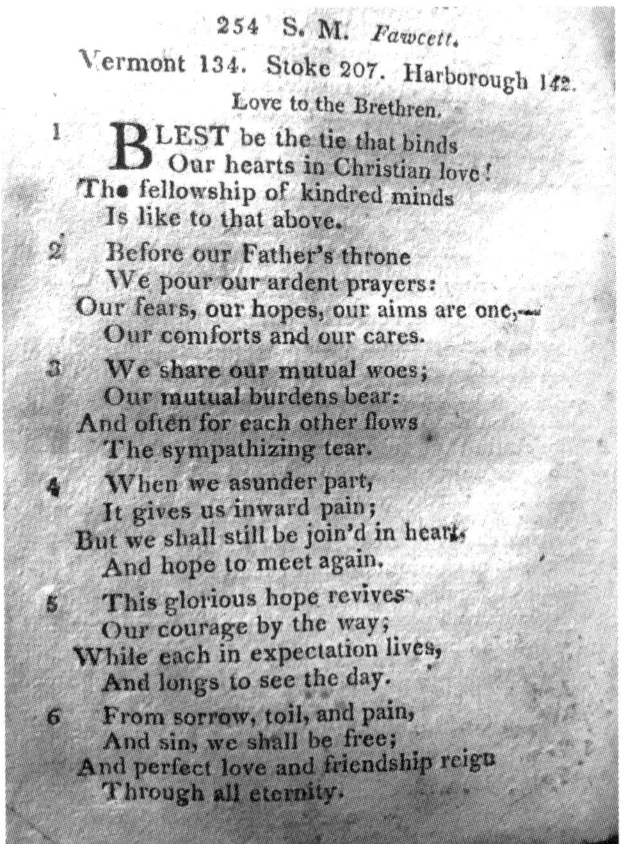

254 S. M. *Fawcett.*
Vermont 134. Stoke 207. Harborough 142.
Love to the Brethren.

1 BLEST be the tie that binds
Our hearts in Christian love!
The fellowship of kindred minds
Is like to that above.

2 Before our Father's throne
We pour our ardent prayers:
Our fears, our hopes, our aims are one,—
Our comforts and our cares.

3 We share our mutual woes;
Our mutual burdens bear:
And often for each other flows
The sympathizing tear.

4 When we asunder part,
It gives us inward pain;
But we shall still be join'd in heart,
And hope to meet again.

5 This glorious hope revives
Our courage by the way;
While each in expectation lives,
And longs to see the day.

6 From sorrow, toil, and pain,
And sin, we shall be free;
And perfect love and friendship reign
Through all eternity.

The hymn "Blest be the tie that binds," from John Fawcett's hymnal

60 John Rippon, *A Selection of Hymns, From the Best Authors*, 4th ed. (London, [1792]), Hymn #254, stanzas 1–3. Fawcett had entitled this hymn "Brotherly Love" (Haykin, "*Blest be the tie that binds,*" 26). Rippon changed the title to "Love to the Brethren."

Fuller, like Fawcett, believed such fellowship to be a rich foretaste of the future, when "perfect love and friendship [will] reign/Thro' all eternity."[61]

As Fuller observed, Steevens himself was also a hymn-writer. According to his memoir in *The Baptist Magazine*, he composed "nearly two thousand hymns." In the words of the unknown author of this memoir, Steevens "took considerable pleasure in versifying."[62] Now, he must have shown Fuller some of the volumes of his handwritten hymns when they met—hence Fuller's request to borrow some of them. His reason for doing so is noteworthy: "Probably some of the notes of your plaintive soul might sound in unison with my feelings." Fuller's perusal of Steevens' hymns would, in his mind, be a further means of cementing their friendship.

There are three additional letters, from 1795 to 1797, in this slice of correspondence between these two eighteenth-century pastors. In these letters Fuller made further reference to his work against Socinianism,[63] as well as his plans to write something on Deism,[64] his ongoing problems with High Calvinism,[65] and the mission to India, in all of

61 Rippon, *A Selection of Hymns*, Hymn #254, stanza 6.

62 "Memoir of the Rev. Thomas Steevens," 87. A few of them were later published in James Upton, *A Collection of Hymns*, 2nd ed. (London, 1815), Hymns #322–348. This hymnal went through three editions by 1818. For help with obtaining this hymnal I am indebted to Chris Fenner, Music & Media Archivist, The Southern Baptist Theological Seminary, Louisville, Kentucky, and Kathryn Sullivan of the Bowld Music Library, Southwestern Baptist Theological Seminary, Fort Worth, Texas.

63 Fuller, Letter to Thomas Steevens, April 14, 1795, in "Extracts from the Late Rev. A. Fuller's Correspondence," 495; *idem*, Letter to Thomas Steevens, June 19, 1795, in "Extracts from the Late Rev. A. Fuller's Correspondence," 495–496.

64 Fuller, Letter to Thomas Steevens, April 14, 1795, in "Extracts from the Late Rev. A. Fuller's Correspondence," 495.

65 Fuller, Letter to Thomas Steevens, April 14, 1795, in "Extracts from the Late Rev. A. Fuller's Correspondence," 495.

which Steevens would have been vitally interested.[66] Regretfully, there do not appear to be any further extant letters of Fuller to Steevens, or vice versa.

A CONCLUDING WORD

So, what do these eight letters reveal? Since Fuller did not live close to Steevens, he used the medium of the letter to cultivate a friendship in which there was a "free and friendly communication of … thoughts" on a host of subjects that concerned them as pastors and that helped to nourish them spiritually. Moreover, these letters bear out Peter Morden's keen observation regarding Fuller that he was "a deep thinker who also felt with a real intensity, … behind the phlegmatic exterior was a man of tender conscience and strong emotions."[67]

---

66 Fuller, Letter to Thomas Steevens, April 14, 1795, in "Extracts from the Late Rev. A. Fuller's Correspondence," 495; *idem*, Letter to Thomas Steevens, February 7, 1797, in "Extracts from the Late Rev. A. Fuller's Correspondence," 496.

67 Morden, *Life and Thought of Andrew Fuller*, 108.

Excursus

A "ONCE INTIMATE FRIEND"

How the friendship of Edward Sharman and Andrew Fuller ended

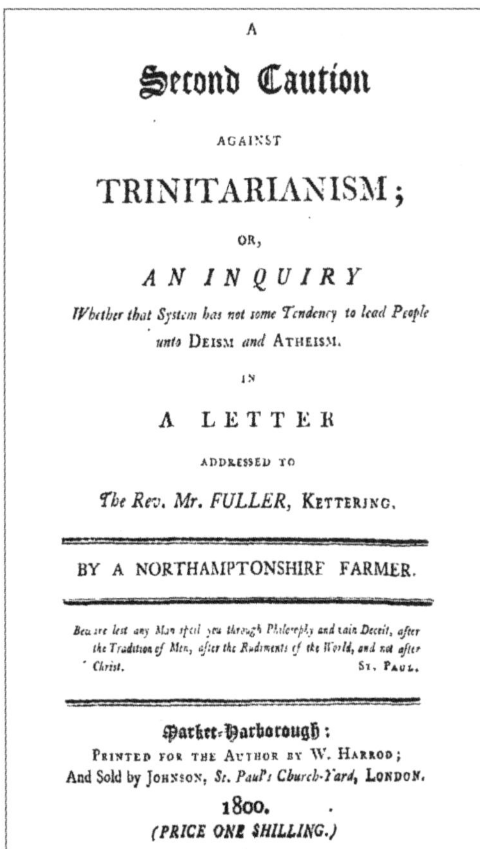

A

Second Caution

AGAINST

TRINITARIANISM;

OR,

AN INQUIRY

Whether that System has not some Tendency to lead People unto DEISM *and* ATHEISM.

IN

A LETTER

ADDRESSED TO

The Rev. Mr. FULLER, KETTERING.

BY A NORTHAMPTONSHIRE FARMER.

Beware lest any Man spoil you through Philosophy and vain Deceit, after the Tradition of Men, after the Rudiments of the World, and not after Christ. ST. PAUL.

Market-Harborough:
PRINTED FOR THE AUTHOR BY W. HARROD;
And Sold by JOHNSON, *St. Paul's Church-Yard,* LONDON.

1800.

(PRICE ONE SHILLING.)

The title page of Edward Sharman,
A Second Caution Against Trinitarianism (1800)

Edward Sharman (fl. 1780–1800) was once a member of the College Street Church in Northampton under the ministry of John Collett Ryland.[68] In 1781, he helped to found Guilsborough Baptist Church in Northamptonshire, and by 1790, he had become the pastor of the Baptist work in the village of Moulton, William Carey's first charge. In the fall of 1792, he was one of the founders of the Baptist Missionary Society.[69] Two years later, though, a day-laborer asked him several questions about the Trinity to which he was unable to provide a satisfactory answer. He later claimed that it was these questions that prompted him to search the Scriptures, to question his previous Trinitarian convictions, and to come to the view that the Socinian perspective better fit the biblical evidence.

When Sharman began to share his newfound views with some of his fellow Baptists, including John Webster Morris (1763–1836), the printer-pastor of Clipstone, Northamptonshire, and Andrew Fuller, he found himself in the midst of what he described as "a dreadful storm." Some called him a heretic, as he had "forsaken the only foundation of the saints," while others, like Morris, considered him "a little deranged."[70]

---

68 For what follows on the career of Sharman, see John Taylor, *History of College Street Church, Northampton* (Northampton: Taylor & Son, The Dryden Press, 1897), 86; John Rippon,"A List of the Particular Baptist Churches in England. 1790" in his ed., *The Baptist Annual Register, for 1790, 1791, 1792, and Part of 1793* (London, 1793), 10; John Rippon,"A List of the Particular Baptist Churches in England. 1794" in his ed., *The Baptist Annual Register, for 1794, 1795, 1796–1797* (London, 1797), 10; Timothy D. Whelan, transcribed and ed., *Baptist Autographs in the John Rylands Library of Manchester, 1741–1845* (Macon, GA: Mercer University Press, 2009), 446.

69 *An Account of the Particular Baptist Society for Propagating the Gospel among the Heathen* in Rippon, ed., *Baptist Annual Register, for 1790, 1791, 1792, and Part of 1793*, 376.

70 Edward Sharman, *A Letter on the Doctrine of the Trinity; addressed to the Baptist Society, at Guilsborough, Northamptonshire* (London: J. Johnson, 1795), 4–9. See also Andrew Fuller, Letter to William Carey, May 2, 1796, in Whelan, transcribed and ed., *Baptist Autographs*, 446.

Sharman's response was to publish a series of four tracts on the subject of the Trinity, in one of which he personally took Morris to task for remarks the latter had written to him in a letter.[71] In another of these pieces he expressed the opinion that his differences with Trinitarians like Fuller were really over a matter "so very trifling," though his subsequent argumentation reveals that this was hardly a tertiary issue for Sharman himself.[72] The final tract, published in 1800, was addressed to Fuller and entitled *A Second Caution Against Trinitarianism; or, An Inquiry Whether that System has not some Tendency to lead People into Deism and Atheism. In a Letter Addressed to The Rev. Mr. Fuller, Kettering.*[73]

In this piece, Sharman did not hesitate to affirm that Christ was a "finite, dependant [*sic*] character" and that only God the Father, being "the only one Almighty God and supreme Governor of all," was worthy of worship. It was, therefore, shameful for Fuller and other Trinitarians to worship Christ, who was but a servant and "inferior messenger," for they were guilty of "dethroning Jehovah from the government of his own world."[74] Far from being a man wise in his understanding of the God of the Scriptures, Fuller was actually ignorant of the Bible, for, Sharman argued, the "mystical plan that Mr. F. had taught me, to reconcile a trinity of persons with the scripture unity of God, I now found to be real polytheism in disguise." In other words, the embrace of

71 Sharman, *A Letter on the Doctrine of the Trinity*, 3–13.

72 Edward Sharman, *A Second Letter on the Doctrine of the Trinity* (Market Harborough: W. Harrod, 1796), 7–9.

73 Edward Sharman, *A Second Caution Against Trinitarianism; or, An Inquiry Whether that System has not some Tendency to lead People into Deism and Atheism. In a Letter Addressed to The Rev. Mr. Fuller, Kettering* (Market Harborough: W. Harrod, 1800).

74 Sharman, *Second Caution Against Trinitarianism*, 7, 9, 11.

Fuller's Trinitarian worship, "instead of deserving the name of promoting Christianity ... will lead me into Deism and Atheism!"—hence the title of this final tract.[75] To add insult to injury, Sharman argued that his new perspective on Christianity was the result of adhering to Fuller's principle that "we must learn what is divine truth immediately from the oracles of God" and we have to "let what God has revealed be the only standard to determine what is right."[76]

Four years earlier, after Sharman had published but one of his four anti-Trinitarian tracts, Fuller had written to William Carey that though "it be a blundering performance, it must be answered."[77] But Fuller never did get around to writing an answer to Sharman. Why? One simple reason was that Fuller was far too busy. Yet, it could also have been out of respect for their past friendship that Fuller held his peace and said nothing. Memories of that friendship would have been awakened when Sharman referred to Fuller as "my once intimate friend, whom I still much respect."[78]

75 Sharman, *Second Caution Against Trinitarianism*, 12, 24, 27.

76 Sharman, *Second Caution Against Trinitarianism*, 27, 33.

77 Andrew Fuller, Letter to William Carey, May 2, 1796, in Whelan, transcribed and ed., *Baptist Autographs*, 446.

78 Sharman, *Second Caution Against Trinitarianism*, 72. Fuller may also have remembered the occasions when they prayed together. See *The Circular Letter from the Baptist Ministers and Messengers Assembled at Northampton, June 4, 5, and 6, 1793* in Rippon, ed., *Baptist Annual Register, for 1794, 1795, 1796–1797*, 31. Truth be told, though, the way that Sharman spoke about Fuller's Trinitarian convictions belied any affirmation of respect.

Chapter 5

"A FOUNTAIN OF SWEETS"

The Friendship of Andrew Fuller and John Ryland & Robert Hall's Mini-discourse on Friendship

> "Friendship, ... under the general culture of reason and religion, ... is one of the fairest productions of the human soil, the cordial of life, the lenitive of our sorrows, and the multiplier of our joys; the source equally of animation and of repose."
>
> —Robert Hall, Jr.,
>
> *Sermon Occasioned by the Death of the Rev. John Ryland* (1825)

The first major biography of Andrew Fuller, which appeared in 1816, the year following Fuller's death, was penned by John Ryland.[1] In the introduction, Ryland stated the following about his relationship with Fuller:

> Most of our common acquaintance are well aware, that I was his oldest and most intimate friend; and though my

1 John Ryland, *The Work of Faith, the Labour of Love, and the Patience of Hope, Illustrated; in the Life and Death of the Reverend Andrew Fuller* (London: Button & Son, 1816).

> removal to Bristol, above twenty years ago, placed us at a distance from each other, yet a constant correspondence was all along maintained; and, to me at least, it seemed a tedious interval, if more than a fortnight elapsed without my receiving a letter from him."[2]

Ryland's assumption of the presidency of Bristol Baptist Academy in 1793 had entailed a move to the West Country from Northampton in the Midlands.[3] No longer physically close to Fuller in Kettering, which was but thirteen miles or so from Northampton, the medium of the letter became the main way that Ryland kept their friendship alive and intact. Thus, for more than twenty years, the two friends faithfully corresponded with one another, and Ryland noted that if he did not hear from Fuller at least once every two weeks, he found it "tedious"—that is, painful and upsetting.[4]

"NEVER WILL MY LOSS BE REPAIRED UPON EARTH!"

Ryland and Fuller first met in 1776, when both of them were young men and were wrestling with a number of extremely important theological issues, especially those that related to the stultifying effects of High Calvinism on their Baptist community and how to pursue the renewal of their churches.[5] Within a year, they were the closest of friends.

2 Ryland, *Life and Death of the Reverend Andrew Fuller*, vi–vii.

3 On Ryland's move to Bristol, see Grant Gordon, "The Call of Dr. John Ryland, Jr.," *The Baptist Quarterly* 34 (1991–1992): 214–227.

4 For this now-obsolete meaning of the word "tedious," see *The Oxford English Dictionary*, s.v.

5 For details of their meeting, see Michael A.G. Haykin, *One Heart and One Soul: John Sutcliff of Olney, His Friends and His Times* (Darlington, Co. Durham, England: Evangelical Press, 1994), 139–141.

And after Fuller moved from Soham to Kettering in 1782, the two of them had frequent opportunities to talk, to pray, and to spend time together.

Their friendship, unbroken till Fuller's death in 1815, was an obvious source of joy to both of them. In the year that he died, Fuller described his relationship with Ryland as a "long and intimate friendship" that he had "lived in, and hoped to die in."[6] And nine days before he died, Fuller asked one last request of Ryland: Would he preach his funeral sermon?

Ryland agreed, though it was no easy task for him to hold back his tears as he spoke.[7] At the beginning of the sermon, Ryland shared his conviction that he had long considered Fuller to be "one of the most conscientious, faithful, and spiritually-minded men on earth" and "perhaps the most judicious and able theological writer that ever belonged to our denomination"—that is, the Particular Baptists of the British Isles and Ireland.[8] Towards the sermon's end, Ryland reminisced about the fact that their friendship had

> never met with one minute's interruption by any one unkind word or thought, of which I have any knowledge. I never had a friend who was so willing to stand by me, even in such services as most others would wish to decline; yet I never

6 Andrew Fuller, *The Admission of Unbaptized Persons to the Lord's Supper Inconsistent with the New Testament* in *Works of the Rev. Andrew Fuller*, 3:508. Fuller did not name Ryland specifically in this passage, but it is clear that Fuller is referring to his friend.

7 See the remarks at the beginning of the sermon: John Ryland, *The Indwelling and Righteousness of Christ No Security against Corporeal Death, but the Source of Spiritual and Eternal Life* (London: W. Button & Son, 1815), 1–2.

8 Ryland, *Indwelling and Righteousness of Christ*, 2–3. For similar remarks to those of Ryland regarding the denominational importance of Fuller, see above, pp. 41–50.

> had a friend who would more faithfully, freely, and affectionately give me warning or reproof, if ever it appeared necessary; or whom I could more readily and freely, and without the least apprehension of giving offence, tell of any fault which I imagined I could see in him. And this I think is the best friendship in the world. For no man is faultless; and true friendship will not be blind to the failings of those we love best; but will rather show itself in an anxious concern to prevent the least appearance of evil in them, or whatever might occasion their good intentions to be misrepresented.
>
> After having lost long ago the venerable Newton and the first Robert Hall, who were the counsellors of my youth; after losing the affectionate Pearce, and the humble and prudent Sutcliff, two other founders of our Mission, this most faithful and judicious friend is also taken from me, and never will my loss be repaired upon earth![9]

Ryland's statement that his friendship with Fuller had "never met with one minute's interruption by one unkind word or thought" speaks volumes about the way these two men treasured their relationship and saw it as a means of human flourishing.

What had initially attracted Fuller and Ryland to one another was the discovery that they shared "a strong attachment to the same religious principles, a decided aversion to the same errors, a predilection for the same authors, ... [and] a concern for the cause of Christ at home and abroad,"[10]

---

9 Ryland, *Indwelling and Righteousness of Christ*, 36–37. On Robert Hall, Sr., Samuel Pearce, and John Sutcliff, see above.

10 Ryland, *Indwelling and Righteousness of Christ*, 35–36.

in particular the American divine Jonathan Edwards and his thought regarding conversion and revival, spirituality, and missions. In other words, they had a fundamental aspect of a good friendship: a union of hearts. In this case, it was a oneness of soul in a shared passion for the glory of Christ and the extension of his kingdom. And yet, as Ryland affirmed in his biography of Fuller, their "intimate friendship did not blind either of us to the defects or faults of the other; but rather showed itself in the freedom of affectionate remark on whatever appeared to be wrong."[11]

"WITHOUT GIVING HIM OFFENCE"

Ryland went on to note that there was only "one religious subject" about which "there was any material difference of judgment" between the two friends.[12] That subject was an extremely volatile one among the eighteenth-century transatlantic Baptist community: the twin issues of open and closed Communion and open and closed membership.[13] The vast majority of pastors and congregations in the Particular Baptist denomination, including Fuller, adhered to a policy of closed membership—that is, only believers baptized by immersion could become members of their local churches—and closed Communion—that is, only believers baptized by immersion could partake of the Lord's Supper in their

11 Ryland, *Life and Death of the Reverend Andrew Fuller*, vii.

12 Ryland, *Life and Death of the Reverend Andrew Fuller*, vii.

13 On these subjects, see B. R. White, "Open and Closed Membership among English and Welsh Baptists," *The Baptist Quarterly* 24 (1971–1972): 330–334, 341; Walter Chantry, "Communion: Open or Closed," *Baptist Reformation Review* 6, no. 4 (Winter 1977): 15–21; Joshua Thompson, "The Communion Controversy and Irish Baptists," *Irish Baptist Historical Society Journal* 20 (1987–1988): 26–35; Roland Burrows, "The Closed Table ... Were Our Forefathers Wrong?," *Evangel* 12, no. 1 (Spring 1994): 23–28.

meeting-houses.[14] This position had been the dominant one within the denomination since the mid-seventeenth century, when it had been given confessional articulation in the *First London Confession of Faith* (1646). This dominance had been challenged by the celebrated John Bunyan (1628–1688) in the 1670s and again a century later by Daniel Turner (1710–1798) of Abingdon, Robert Robinson (1735–1790) of Cambridge, and John Ryland's father, John Collett Ryland, but the majority of the denomination, like Fuller, remained committed to closed Communion.[15]

Like his father, John Ryland was of the persuasion that both the Lord's Supper and membership in the local church should be open to all Christians, regardless of whether or not they had been baptized as believers. He was thus committed to a policy of both open Communion and open membership. When Ryland was the pastor of the College Lane Church in Northampton, for instance, one of the leading deacons of the church, a certain Thomas Trinder, did not receive believer's baptism until six years after he had been appointed deacon.[16] Fuller would never have tolerated such a situation in

---

14 For Fuller's views, see *Thoughts on Open Communion* (1800) in *Works of the Rev. Andrew Fuller*, 3:503–506; *Strict Communion in the Mission Church at Serampore* (1814) in *Works of the Rev. Andrew Fuller*, 3:507; *The Admission of Unbaptized Persons to the Lord's Supper Inconsistent with the New Testament* in *Works of the Rev. Andrew Fuller*, 3:508–515.

15 For the seventeenth-century controversy involving Bunyan, see Michael A.G. Haykin with C. Jeffrey Robinson, "Particular Baptist Debates about Communion and Hymn-Singing" in Michael A.G. Haykin and Mark Jones, eds., *'Drawn into Controversie': Reformed Theological Diversity and Debates Within Seventeenth-Century British Puritanism*, Reformed Historical Theology, vol. 17 (Göttingen: Vandenhoeck & Ruprecht, 2011), 285–296; and for the eighteenth-century debate, see Robert W. Oliver, *History of the English Calvinistic Baptists 1771–1892: From John Gill to C. H. Spurgeon* (Edinburgh; Carlisle, PA: The Banner of Truth Trust, 2006), 58–88.

16 Gordon, "Call of Dr. John Ryland," 217.

the church at Kettering. But Ryland and Fuller were secure enough in their friendship to disagree about this controversial subject and not have it destroy their friendship.

The only time that this theological difference really came close to disturbing their bond was in connection with the Baptist Missionary Society's ecclesial practice at Serampore, India.[17] Headed by Carey, Marshman, and William Ward (1769–1823)—all of whom were friends of Ryland and Fuller—this mission adopted a policy of open Communion in 1805. Writing to Fuller that year, the Serampore missionaries informed him that they had come to the belief that "no one has a right to debar a true Christian from the Lord's table, nor refuse to communicate with a real Christian in commemorating the death of their common Lord, without being guilty of a breach of the Law of Love." They went on to affirm: "We cannot doubt, whether a Watts, an Edwards, a Brainerd, a Doddridge, a Whitefield, did right in partaking of the Lord's Supper, though really unbaptized, or whether they had the presence of God at the Lord's Table?"

Fuller was deeply disturbed by this reasoning and the decision made by the Serampore missionaries, and he exerted all of his powers of influence and reasoning to convince them to embrace closed Communion, which they eventually did in 1811. Ryland, though, was not slow to criticize this reversal of policy. But, as he later said of his disagreement with Fuller: "I repeatedly expressed myself more freely and strongly to him, than I did to any man in England; yet without giving him

17 For the quotes in this paragraph, see E. Daniel Potts, "'I throw away the guns to preserve the ship': A Note on the Serampore Trio," *The Baptist Quarterly* 20 (1963–1964): 115–117.

offence."[18] Neither did Carey take offense at Fuller. When he heard of Fuller's death in 1815, he wrote almost immediately to Ryland and told him: "I loved him very sincerely. There was scarcely another man on the earth to whom I could so completely lay open my heart as I could to him."[19]

When Fuller lay dying in April of 1815, he was asked if he wanted to see Ryland, his oldest living friend in England. His response was terse: "He can do me no good."[20] His reply seems to be an odd statement, lacking in appreciation for what their friendship had meant to the two men. But it needs to be understood in context. In his final letter to Ryland, Fuller had begun by saying: "We have enjoyed much together, which I hope will prove an earnest of greater enjoyment in another world. … [There] I trust we shall meet, and part no more."[21] Clearly, his feelings about his friendship with Ryland had undergone no alteration whatsoever. In the light of his impending death, however, there was only one friendship which he knew to be utterly needful in that moment: his friendship with the triune God—Father, Son, and Holy Spirit.

It is all too human to regard our views about tertiary, even secondary, matters as far more important than they actually are and to attempt to squeeze our friends into our mold of thinking when it comes to such issues. Fuller and Ryland, on the other hand, genuinely knew how to give each other space to disagree on what a significant number of their Baptist acquaintances regarded as an essential issue.

---

18 Ryland, *Life and Death of the Rev. Andrew Fuller*, viii.

19 William Carey, Letter to John Ryland, November 15, 1815, in Terry G. Carter, ed., *The Journal and Selected Letters of William Carey* (Macon, GA: Smyth & Helwys Publishing, 2000), 199. Spelling modernized.

20 Ryland, *Life and Death of the Rev. Andrew Fuller*, 356.

21 Ryland, *Indwelling and Righteousness of Christ*, 33.

Robert Hall, Jr.
(Wikimedia Commons)

"THE CORDIAL OF LIFE, THE LENITIVE OF OUR SORROWS, AND THE MULTIPLIER OF OUR JOYS"

Ryland outlived Fuller by a decade. When he died in May of 1825, his friend Robert Hall, Jr., preached his funeral sermon. Hall based this sermon upon a specific phrase from John 21:7, "That disciple whom Jesus loved" (KJV). More than half of it was taken up with a sketch of Ryland's Christian character and the significance of his life. The other half was equally divided between attention to the Johannine passage and a long introduction that acted as a mini-discourse on the nature of friendship.

Hall began with the charge alleged by unbelievers that it is "a defect in the morality of the gospel, that it neglects to inculcate patriotism and friendship."[22] Hall first made a few remarks as to why he felt that this charge was based on a misunderstanding of the relationship between Christianity and love of one's own country. He then turned to the question of friendship. He readily admitted that Christ "did not prescribe the cultivation of friendship" but did admonish his followers to pursue a virtuous life, which has proven to be the best of all soils for the flourishing of friendship. Virtues such as "humility, forbearance, gentleness, kindness," and empathy were "the best preparation" for the development of friendship. Where such exist, "friendship will be the natural result."[23]

Even as happiness cannot be prescribed, Hall emphasized, so friendship cannot be contained within "the fetters of prescriptions." If one sought to lay down detailed instructions to be followed in one's friendships, Hall argued,

> endless embarrassments would arise in determining at what period the relation shall commence; whether with one or with more; and at what stage, in the progress of mutual attraction, at what point, the feelings of reciprocal

---

22 Robert Hall, Jr., *A Sermon Occasioned by the Death of the Rev. John Ryland, D.D., Preached at the Baptist Meeting, Broadmead, Bristol, June 5, 1825*, in *The Works of the Rev. Robert Hall, A.M.*, ed. Olinthus Gregory, 2nd ed. (London: Holdsworth and Ball, 1832), 1:371.

23 Hall, Jr., *Sermon Occasioned by the Death of the Rev. John Ryland* in *Works of the Rev. Robert Hall*, ed. Gregory, 1:373–374.

> regard shall be deemed to reach the maturity which entitles them to the sacred name of friendship. ... he who should undertake to prescribe to the subtle and mysterious impulses which invite susceptible minds to friendship, would find himself engaged in an attempt as hopeless, as to regulate the motions of the air which bloweth where it listeth.[24]

However, Hall showed no reluctance to sing the praises of friendship: "Under the general culture of reason and religion, it is one of the fairest productions of the human soil, the cordial of life, the lenitive of our sorrows, and the multiplier of our joys; the source equally of animation and of repose."[25]

Human nature is also so constituted that it needs another to share its joys. In Hall's words: "The satisfaction derived from surveying the most beautiful scenes of nature, or the most exquisite productions of art, is so far from being complete, that it almost turns into uneasiness, when there is none with whom we can share it."[26]

It is noteworthy that this common appreciation of beauty was not shared by Fuller. Ryland told the story of Fuller's first visit to Oxford. A friend—it might have been James Hinton (1761–1823), pastor of the Baptist cause in the university town[27]—took him around to see the major

---

24 Hall, Jr., *Sermon Occasioned by the Death of the Rev. John Ryland* in *Works of the Rev. Robert Hall*, ed. Gregory, 1:374–375.

25 Hall, Jr., *Sermon Occasioned by the Death of the Rev. John Ryland* in *Works of the Rev. Robert Hall*, ed. Gregory, 1:375–376.

26 Hall, Jr., *Sermon Occasioned by the Death of the Rev. John Ryland* in *Works of the Rev. Robert Hall*, ed. Gregory, 1:377.

27 On Hinton, see Michael A.G. Haykin, *"Accounted Worthy to Bear in My Body the Marks of the Lord Jesus": James Hinton, the Persecution of English Dissent, and the Woodstock Riot* (Louisville, KY: The Andrew Fuller Center for Baptist Studies,

buildings and to admire their architectural beauty. Fuller, though, was unmoved, and at one point said to his friend, "Brother, I think there is one question, which, after all that has been written on it, has not yet been well answered." At his friend's inquiry as to what that might be, Fuller replied, "The question is, What is justification? ... That inquiry is far more to me than all these fine buildings."[28]

Of course, this lack of desire to discuss Oxford's celebrated buildings, this "sweet City with her dreaming spires,"[29] did not mean Fuller had no appreciation of friendship. In fact, this anecdote reveals the very opposite: Fuller was eager to spend time in his friend's company, but just not in looking at buildings! And Ryland tells us that they immediately went back to the friend's house to discuss the theological locus of justification.

Hall also appreciated friendship because of its usefulness for living the Christian life:

> He who has made the acquisition of a judicious and sympathizing friend, may be said to have doubled his mental resources: by associating an equal, perhaps a superior mind, with his own, he has provided the means of strengthening his reason, of perfecting his counsels, of discerning and correcting his errors. He can have recourse at all times to the judgement and assistance of one, who

---

2018) and *The Diary of James Hinton (1761–1823)*, ed. Chance Faulkner (Peterborough, ON: H&E Publishing, 2020).

28 Ryland, *Life and Death of the Reverend Andrew Fuller*, 574–575.

29 Matthew Arnold, "Thyrsis: A Monody, to Commemorate the Author's Friend, Arthur Hugh Clough, who died at Florence, 1861," line 19 (https://www.bartleby.com/254/95.html; accessed June 3, 2021).

> with the same power of discernment with himself, comes to the decision of a question with a mind neither harassed with the perplexities, nor heated with the passions, which so frequently obscure the perception of our true interests. Next to the immediate guidance of God by his Spirit, the counsel and encouragement of virtuous and enlightened friends afford the most powerful aid, in the encounter of temptation and in the career of duty.[30]

Hall did not mention the friendship between the subject of this funeral sermon—namely, Ryland—and John Newton in this regard, but surely that friendship illustrated Hall's point here.

Ryland turned to Newton frequently for help in thinking through the challenges he faced as a pastor, father, and president of a seminary. In the above paragraph, Hall's concluding sentence is quite remarkable. Whatever he has in mind by the phrase "the immediate guidance of God by his Spirit"—the adjective "immediate" suggests that he is not thinking of the Scriptures—he certainly assigned to friendship a vital role in defending the believer against sin and encouraging him or her to do what is pleasing to God. Hall elaborated by emphasizing that when tempted by sin we need to have in view not only "the eye of Omniscience," but also "the remembrance that our conduct is subject to the scrutiny of friends."[31] Hall went on to depict friendship as a place of honesty and transparency, where one is "accustomed to lay open the interior

30 Hall, Jr., *Sermon Occasioned by the Death of the Rev. John Ryland* in *Works of the Rev. Robert Hall*, ed. Gregory, 1:377–378.

31 Hall, Jr., *Sermon Occasioned by the Death of the Rev. John Ryland* in *Works of the Rev. Robert Hall*, ed. Gregory, 1:378–379.

of his character and the most retired secrets of his heart," so that a friend can speak into your life, honestly reproving error and warmly encouraging virtue.[32] Of course, friends cannot be together all of the time. But even this absence can enhance one's friendship. In Hall's words, when one's friends are absent, the remembrance of this "mutual attachment of kindred spirits" has a distinct pleasure, "refreshing and exhilarating the mind."[33]

As Hall drew this mini-discourse to a close, and before he launched into an exegetical consideration of the Johannine text that was the subject of his sermon, he once again lauded the value of friendship:

> It is a treasure possessed, when it is not employed; a reserve of strength, ready to be called into action when most needed; a fountain of sweets, to which we may continually repair, whose waters are inexhaustible.[34]

In our less prosaic age, it is tempting to take Hall's depiction of friendship here as "a fountain of sweets, ... whose waters are inexhaustible" as sheer hyperbole. To do so, in my mind, would be to confirm, albeit in a small degree, the observation with which this book began, namely, that we as occidental evangelicals give little thought to the subject of friendship.

32 Hall, Jr., *Sermon Occasioned by the Death of the Rev. John Ryland* in *Works of the Rev. Robert Hall*, ed. Gregory, 1:379.

33 Hall, Jr., *Sermon Occasioned by the Death of the Rev. John Ryland* in *Works of the Rev. Robert Hall*, ed. Gregory, 1:379–380.

34 Hall, Jr., *Sermon Occasioned by the Death of the Rev. John Ryland* in *Works of the Rev. Robert Hall*, ed. Gregory, 1:380.

The term "sweet," of course, had a lineage in the affective spirituality of John Calvin (1509–1564), the Puritans, and especially Jonathan Edwards.[35] As a spiritual term in this Reformed tradition, it and its cognates, like "sweetness," speak of the enflaming of the affections such that one's life is oriented towards the glory of the triune God and all that God loves. Its "waters are inexhaustible" only because true friendship has an eternal dimension. Friendships in Christ have "an endless duration," Hall went to emphasize, and when the heavens and this world are no more, they will "spring fresh from the ashes of the universe." Such friendships that have piety and true religion for their basis "will ere long be transplanted, in order to adorn the paradise of God."[36]

All of this is high praise indeed for the role that friendship can play in the Christian life and, in the light of eternity, not at all exaggeration.

---

35 See, for instance, I. John Hesselink, "Calvin, Theologian of Sweetness," *Calvin Theological Journal* 37 (2002): 318–332; and Leonard I. Sweet, "The Laughter of One: Sweetness and Light in Franklin and Edwards" in Barbara B. Oberg and Harry S. Stout, eds., *Benjamin Franklin, Jonathan Edwards, and the Representation of American Culture* (New York; Oxford: Oxford University Press, 1993), 114–133.

36 Hall, Jr., *Sermon Occasioned by the Death of the Rev. John Ryland* in *Works of the Rev. Robert Hall*, ed. Gregory, 1:380.

The jacket cover of The Iliad of Homer, retold by Barbara Leonie Picard (London: Oxford University Press, 1960)

Afterword

Dominating my childhood was the world of Homer's *The Iliad*. When I was seven or eight, I was given—whether it was a birthday or Christmas present, I cannot recall—*The Iliad of Homer*, retold by Barbara Leonie Picard (1917–2011). Its fabulous illustrations by Joan Kiddell-Monroe (1908–1972), coupled with Picard's marvelous retelling, gripped my young mind and heart.

Looking back, I am certain that the Homeric statements about friendship, including the lines of Homer's poem that tell of Achilles' love for Patroclus that I cited in Chapter 1 (rendered by Picard as "Patroclus is dead, whom I honoured above all men and loved more than my life"[1]), helped to stir within my heart a hunger for friendship. I feel that even as I have been surrounded by a love for history since my earliest memories, so I have been shaped by a passion for and fascination with friendship.

This passion and fascination have shaped a significant portion of my scholarship, from my doctoral work on the pneumatology of the group of friends known as the Cappadocian Fathers—Basil of Caesarea, Gregory of Nazianzus, Gregory of Nyssa (c. 335–c. 395), and Amphilochius of Iconium (c. 340–c. 395/400)[2]— to what essentially, in retrospect, felt like a second doctoral thesis that was published

1 *The Iliad of Homer*, retold by Barbara Leonie Picard (London: Oxford University Press, 1960), 150–151.

2 Published as *The Spirit of God: The Exegesis of 1 and 2 Corinthians in the Pneumatomachian Controversy of the Fourth Century* (Leiden: E. J. Brill, 1994).

as *One Heart and One Soul: John Sutcliff of Olney, His Friends and His Times*.[3] More recently, when I was asked to write a popular biography of William Carey, I was very conscious that there already existed a huge number of biographies of the iconic missionary, so I focused it upon Carey's friendships, an area that had not really been developed in Carey scholarship.[4]

This research and writing have convinced me that friendship is not merely a subject of personal interest but is vital for the advance of God's reign in the world. I believe firmly that whenever God has done great things in the history of the church, he has done it through a group of friends, a band of brothers and sisters. As Christopher Anderson (1782–1852), a Scottish Baptist leader who was among Fuller's circle of friends, once remarked:

> [I]n order to much good being done, co-operation, the result of undissembled love, is absolutely necessary; and I think that if God in his tender mercy would take me as one of but a very few whose hearts he will unite as the heart of one man—since all the watchmen cannot see eye to eye—might I be but one of a little band of brothers who should do so, and who should leave behind them a proof of how much may be accomplished in consequence of the union of only a few upon earth in spreading Christianity, oh how should I rejoice and be glad! In order to such a union, however, I am satisfied that the cardinal virtues, and a share of what may be considered as substantial

3 *One Heart and One Soul: John Sutcliff of Olney, His Friends and His Times* (Darlington, Co. Durham, England: Evangelical Press, 1994).

4 *The Missionary Fellowship of William Carey* (Orlando, FL: Reformation Trust, 2018).

> excellence of character, are absolutely necessary, and hence the importance of the religion which we possess being of that stamp which will promote these. Such a union in modern times existed in [Andrew] Fuller, [John] Sutcliff, [Samuel] Pearce, [William] Carey, and [John] Ryland. They were men of self-denying habits, dead to the world, to fame, and to popular applause, of deep and extensive views of divine truth, and they had such an extended idea of what the Kingdom of Christ ought to have been in the nineteenth century, that they, as it were, vowed and prayed, and gave themselves no rest.[5]

This is a truth that we who are evangelicals have forgotten. My prayer is that this book may be a vehicle of much-needed remembrance!

5 Christopher Anderson, Letter, September 7, 1822, in Hugh Anderson, *The Life and Letters of Christopher Anderson* (Edinburgh: W. P. Kennedy, 1854), 379.

Appendix

LEMUEL COVELL AND HIS LETTER ON "CHRISTIAN FRIENDSHIP" (1801)[1]

Mark E. Joubert and Michael A.G. Haykin

Baptist usage of the term "friendship" in the long eighteenth century was definitely broader than the focus it has received in this book. Consider this text on Christian friendship that

1 Mark E. Joubert, an M.Div. student at Southern Baptist Theological Seminary, originally edited and formatted the entire text of Lemuel Covell's letter on Christian friendship, which was written at the behest of the Shaftsbury Baptist Association in 1801. Michael Haykin then made some selections and with Mark Joubert added the introductory comments. Scripture citations have been modernized or, in some cases, added. Words and Scripture citations within square brackets indicate additions to the text. The punctuation has been modernized, and some of the paragraphs have been combined. The original is Lemuel Covell, "Corresponding Letter" in *Minutes of the Shaftsbury Baptist Association Held at Galway, The Third and Fourth of June, 1801: Together With Their Circular and Corresponding Letters* (Troy, NY: Robert Moffitt & Co., 1801), 15–19. See also Deidamia C. Brown, *Memoir of the Late Rev. Lemuel Covell* (Brandon: Telegraph Office, 1839), 45–48, which contains most of this letter.

was written in 1801 by the American Baptist Lemuel Covell (1764–1806). Covell was a pastor and occasional missionary to the Iroquoian-speaking Tuscarora First Nation, who lived around the Great Lakes and were part of the Six Nations Confederacy. Converted in Lower Canada before 1789, Covell subsequently became a Baptist and in 1792 preached his first sermon at the Third Baptist Church in Galway on what was then the New York frontier.

Under his preaching, there was a genuine measure of revival in 1794, and two years later he was ordained as the pastor of the Second Baptist Church in Providence, New York. Covell had a notable ministry among the churches of the Shaftsbury Baptist Association, which encompassed congregations from New York, Vermont, and Massachusetts.

Covell successfully established a home missions society with the goal of advancing the gospel along the frontier and into Upper Canada. On one trip to Upper Canada (i.e., Ontario), he baptized some thirty people at Long Point and helped organize one of the first Baptist congregations in that region at Charlotteville. On another trip to Upper Canada in 1806, he succumbed to typhus fever; he was buried in the Baptist cemetery at what is now Beamsville, Ontario. He has been described as "the most outstanding personality" among the early Baptist missionaries in Upper Canada, a man who was "intense and energetic" and "utterly selfless" in the spread of the gospel.[2]

2 Stuart Ivison and Fred Rosser, *The Baptists in Upper and Lower Canada before 1820* (1956, Toronto: University of Toronto Press, 1963), 67–70, *passim*. For Covell's life and ministry, see especially Brown, *Memoir of the Late Rev. Lemuel Covell*. This memoir contains, in addition to the letter on friendship, extracts from Covell's diary, as well as a hymn entitled "The Triumphs of Grace in the Wilderness" (*Memoir of the Late Rev. Lemuel Covell*, 59–61).

For Covell, "friendship" expresses the relationship between all genuine Christians and their God. As revealed by the selections that follow, Covell grounded Christian friendship in the perichoretic relations between the members of the Godhead in a way that echoes the reflections on the Trinity by such Christian authors as Augustine and Jonathan Edwards.[3]

The hymn, composed by Covell, outlined God's salvific work through Christ and its long-term impact on what Covell called "the dark wilderness" of the North American frontier:

> No more shall the sound of the war-whoop be heard,
> The ambush and slaughter, no longer be fear'd;
> The tomahawk, buried, shall rust in the ground,
> While peace and good will to the nations abound.

In the context of the hymn, Covell seems to be describing the future state when "all shall submit and rejoice" in Christ's rule, when "white and red shall, in friendship be join'd" and "united in praise, / One vast hallelujah, triumphant, shall raise!" The hope of interracial friendship is notable, though nothing is said about the violence of the European cultures in North America towards the First Nations.

3 John Collett Ryland anticipated Covell's approach in his *The Beauty of Social Religion*, Circular Letter of the Northamptonshire Baptist Association (Northampton: T. Dicey, 1777), 2–3: "In treating on the nature of a Gospel Church, we will endeavour to keep in mind one peculiar idea of it, which must render it one of the most lovely and desirable things in the world, (viz.) that it is a state of gracious and refined friendship, grounded on a cordial love to God and to each other. Spiritual friendship is a pleasing attraction of the heart towards the beautiful and good qualities which we esteem, and the amiable image of God we admire in true Christians—which produces a mutual inclination between two or more persons to promote each other's holiness and happiness. This spiritual friendship is the union of souls by means of vital holiness, which is the common cement or bond of their mutual and ardent affection. In treating of a Gospel Church, under the pleasing idea of a state of rational, moral, and divine friendship, we consider its materials, constitution and form, the dignity, order, officers, worship, spirit and uses of such a society." I (Michael Haykin) am indebted to Garrett Walden, one of my doctoral students at Southern Baptist Theological Seminary, for drawing my attention to this specific text.

Christian Friendship

Christian friendship is not that sordid principle which inclines the rich in this world to look with affected complaisance on the sons of wealth nor that mercenary principle which confines its good will to the hand of benediction. It is not that perfidious principle which pretends great respect for those whom it would gladly employ as instruments; nor that selfish principle, which bestows gifts with the sole design of effecting its own purposes. It is not that party spirit, which circumscribes itself to those of its own caste; nor [that] contracted spirit, which delights only in those of its own family. It is not that versatile spirit, which is easily attracted by new objects, but can retain no lasting attachment to any, consequently is variable, fickle, and unstable; nor is it that blind, bigoted spirit, which never discovers any imperfections in the objects of its delight, and therefore maintains an obstinate attachment, supported neither by reason nor friendship, but by stubborn predilection. But,

That friendship which is the subject of this letter, is that divine principle which, by assimilating our souls to the great eternal Source of all *true* friendship, knits and cements them [in] the most indissoluble union. This is, undoubtedly, what the great Apostle means by the "unity of the Spirit" (Eph. 4:3), by the "fellowship of the Spirit" (Phil. 2:1), and by that oneness, by which "Christ is all and in all" (Col. 3:11), but, more particularly, that charity delineated in 1 Corinthians 13. To trace this glorious principle to its exalted source is a work at once pleasing, interesting and sublime. In this delightful stretch of contemplation, we have the infallible Word for our guide. Let us listen a moment to its language.

"The Lord possessed me in the beginning of his way, before his works of old. I was set up from everlasting, before ever the earth was. ... Then I was before him, as one brought up with him. And I was daily his delight, rejoicing always before him. Rejoicing in the habitable parts of his earth, and my delights were with the sons of men" [Prov. 8:22–23, 30–31]. "And now, Father, glorify thou me with thine own self, with the glory which I had with thee before the world was" [John 17:5]. "As thou, Father, art in me, and I in thee" [John 17:21]. Here we have the most emphatical description of true friendship and are led to see that it has its source in the ever-blessed God, and therefore, that its nature is heavenly and divine.

We learn also, from the Scriptures of truth, that the adorable medium through which this divine principle has made its appearance in our world, is the blessed Immanuel. The Father "so loved the world, that he has given his only begotten Son, that whosoever believes in him should not perish, but have everlasting life" [John 3:16]. If any man loves the Son, the Father will love him, and they will come and take up their abode with him [cf. John 14:23]. And thus, every Christian is united to God, by the same divine principle which unites the Father and the Son. "That they all may be one, as thou, Father, are in me, and I in thee; that they also may be one in us. ... And the glory which thou gavest me I have given them; that they may be one, even as we are one; I in them, and thou in me, that they may be made perfect in one; and that the world may know that thou hast sent me, and hast loved them as thou hast loved me" [John 17:21–23]. What could be more expressive? Will not this language of the blessed Jesus justify the Apostle in saying that we are made partakers of the divine nature (2 Pet. 1:4)?

Having thus, by tracing this heavenly stream to its source, discovered its nature, let us, for a moment, turn our attention to its progress and effects. The eternal Father and his dearly beloved Son, being united by that Holy Spirit of love, union, and friendship, which dwells in and proceeds from both, and by which they mutually dwell in and are delighted with each other, have early devised a plan which brings into view the exercise and progress of that ever-living, ever-acting principle, in all its beneficent effects. This glorious plan, called by some the covenant of grace, by others the covenant of redemption, and is emphatically both, as it is a gracious plan to redeem sinners, embraces the elect of God, with all the means of their salvation; and discloses that eternal friendship which the Father had towards them, in his dear Son, before the world began; and exhibits its progress through all the divine dispensations, till it shall appear complete in their consummation in glory. ...

The effects of divine friendship are: a complete reconciliation to God, produced in the hearts of the most obdurate and rebellious sinners, by the powerful operation of divine love shed abroad in their hearts by his Holy Spirit, by which that enmity of heart is removed, by which they were opposed to God and his law, and full of malice and hatred one against another; their being united in the delightful bonds of love and fellowship, and mutually engaged to seek and promote each other's good; and that holy communion with God and his people, which every Christian enjoys, in a greater or smaller degree, by the sweet influences of the holy Comforter, the Spirit of Truth. ...

Hence, we see, dear brethren, that Christian friendship is the same in nature with that love which dwelt in the bosom of the Father towards his only begotten Son, and his people in him, which arose in the breast of the adorable God-man, first towards his heavenly Father, and then towards his Bride, who was chosen in him before the world began [Eph.1:4]. We also see that it is the same spirit of union by which the great eternal Father dwelt in and glorified his dear Son with his own self, by which the blessed Immanuel dwelt in the bosom of the Father, before his works of old, and was daily his delight; that by which the Lord Jesus Christ dwells in his people, and the Father in him, by which they are made perfect in one. God in Christ—Christ in his people—his people in him. This, dear brethren, is that threefold cord, which neither life nor death, time nor eternity, sin nor holiness, can dissolve. This is that immutable, all-powerful principle, which, in its progress, has run through all the divine dispensations, and effected all its beneficent purposes, in defiance of all opposition. [This is] that which, in its effects, slays the enmity of our hearts, reconciles us to God, and unites us together in the unity of the Spirit and bond of peace.

This view of the subject exhibits the great Jehovah as the inexhaustible fountain of true friendship—the blessed Jesus as the friend of sinners, who has laid down his life for them—and the Holy Spirit as that glorious teacher, who will inculcate the same principle in their hearts. …

Let us then, dear brethren, unite our efforts to cultivate union and harmony while we are passing through this vale of tears, till we arrive in that upper and better world, where divine friendship reigns, in all its unfading glory, and sheds its benign influences on all those happy millions who surround the throne of God and the Lamb forever.

FOR FURTHER READING

As David Konstan notes in his book on friendship in antiquity, "Virtually everyone who writes on friendship, ancient or modern, is given to remarking that it has not, until recently, invited substantial attention from scholars." And among the areas needing study in this regard, he specifies Christian friendship.[1] What follows are a few excellent works on friendship, both popular and scholarly, in addition to what I have cited in this book.

Anonymous, "The Gift of Friendship," *The Royal Bank Letter* 66, no. 4 (July/August 1985) (http://www.rbc.com/aboutus/letter/jul_aug1985.html; accessed June 6, 2021).

John P. Bequette, *Christian Friendship: Engaging the Tradition, Transforming the Culture* (Eugene, OR: Cascade Books, 2019).

1 David Konstan, *Friendship in the Classical World* (Cambridge: Cambridge University Press, 1997), 174, 176.

Hugh Black, *Friendship* (1898, Guelph, ON: Joshua Press; Fenstanton, England: Leith Books, 2008).

Hugh Blair, "Sermon LXVII: On Friendship" in *Sermons* (New York: Harper & Brothers, 1859), 466–471.

David E. Briones, "*Why Can't We Be Friends? Paul and Aristotle on Friendship*" in Joseph R. Dodson and David E. Briones, eds., *Paul and the Giants of Philosophy: Reading the Apostle in Greco-Roman Context* (Downers Grove, IL: IVP Academic, 2019), 36–49.

Edward Carpenter, ed., *An Anthology of Friendship* (Albert & Charles Boni, 1935).

Cicero, *On Old Age and On Friendship*, trans. Frank O. Copley (Ann Arbor, MI: The University of Michigan Press, 1967), 45–90.

Howard Griffith, "Richard Baxter and the 'Godly Brotherhood' of Christian Friendship," *The Banner of Truth* 247 (April 1984): 20–29, 32; 248 (May 1984): 25–28.

Michael A.G. Haykin and Joel R. Beeke, *How Should We Develop Biblical Friendship?* (Grand Rapids, MI: Reformation Heritage Books, 2015).

Samuel Hopkins, *A Discourse on Christian Friendship* in *The Works of Samuel Hopkins* (1865, New York; London: Garland Publishing, Inc., 1987), 2:625–700.

David Konstan, *Friendship in the Classical World* (Cambridge: Cambridge University Press, 1997).

C. S. Lewis, *The Four Loves* (New York: HarperCollins, 2017).

Martin E. Marty, *Friendship* (Allen, TX: Argus Communications, 1980).

Gilbert Meilaender, *Friendship: A Study in Theological Ethics* (Notre Dame, IN: University of Notre Dame Press, 1981).

Rudolf Schnackenburg, *The Friend We Have in Jesus,* trans. Mark A. Christian (Louisville, KY: Westminster John Knox Press, 1997).

David Schwartz, *Aquinas on Friendship* (Oxford: Oxford University Press, 2007).

Suzanne Stern-Giller and Gary M. Gurtler, eds., *Ancient and Medieval Concepts of Friendship* (Albany, NY: State University of New York Press, 2014).

Jerry and Mary White, *Friends & Friendship: The Secrets of Drawing Closer* (Colorado Springs, CO: NavPress, 1982).

ACKNOWLEDGEMENTS

I am deeply thankful to God for friends in my life, especially the five Canadian brothers to whom this book is dedicated. I am also grateful to God for the privilege of serving him and his people at The Southern Baptist Theological Seminary, and in particular, I am deeply indebted to Drs. Matthew J. Hall and Hershael W. York for their providing me with the context in which to research and write books like this one.

Thanks also to Dr. Grant Gordon for drawing my attention to certain infelicities in the text and to Dr. Rebecca Rine and Chance Faulkner for shepherding this book through to publication. Some of the material in this book has seen print before, and for permission to use this material in this book, I am grateful to:

Reformation Heritage Books: Parts of Chapter 1 appeared in Michael A.G. Haykin and Joel R. Beeke, *How Should We Develop Biblical Friendship?* (2015).

Joshua Press: Parts of Chapter 3 appeared in Michael A.G. Haykin, *Eighteenth-Century Evangelicals as Spiritual Mentors: "Love is unfurled"* (2018), Chapter 6.

Lexham Press: Chapter 4 originally appeared in *The Spirit of Holiness: Reflections on Biblical Spirituality*, ed. Terry Delaney and Roger D. Duke (2020). Reprinted with permission.

Reformation Fellowship

Reformation Fellowship is a global movement of pastors, ministers, students, missionaries and believers who share a common vision: to see reformation in Christ's church worldwide.

Through publications, theological input, biblical resources, podcasts, webinars, and every other means at our disposal, we desire to create a culture of gospel integrity and gather a global movement of believers under the gospel banner of Christ.

Join the fellowship:
reffellowship.org

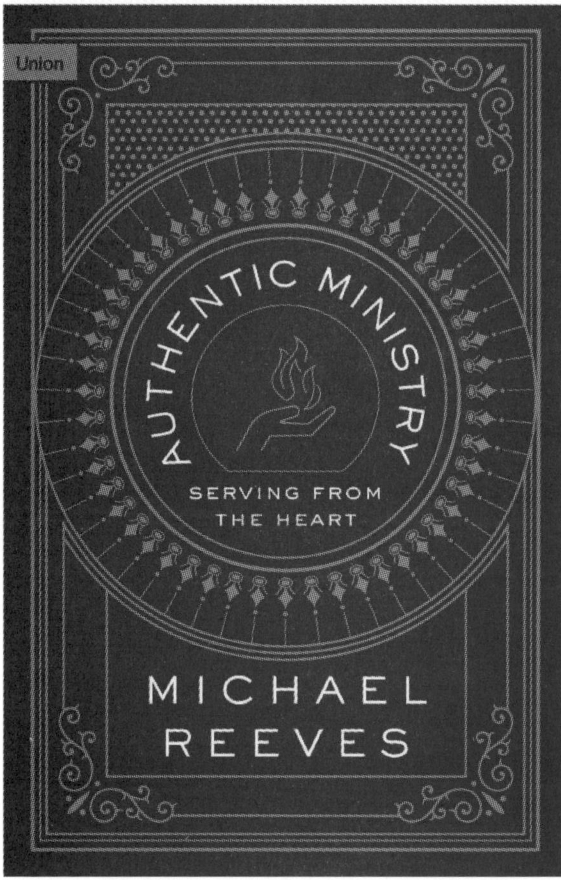

Authentic ministry is not simply a matter of mastering professional skills or of endlessly pouring oneself out in works of service. Rather, it springs from joyful union with Christ. *Authentic Ministry* offers practical guidance and spiritual nourishment for all who serve the church. Each of the nine chapters orients readers to the "one thing [that] is necessary" (cf. Luke 10:42)—abiding in Christ—while asking and answering questions both simple and profound: What is prayer? How should I respond to suffering? Who is my friend? What is theology? What does it mean to love? This short volume originated as a series of talks delivered to various assemblies of students, pastors-in-training, and church leaders in the UK and beyond.